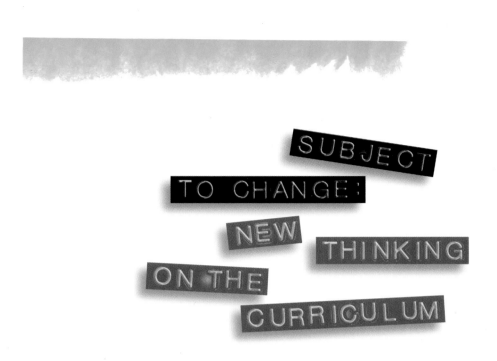

SUBJECT TO CHANGE: NEW THINKING ON THE CURRICULUM

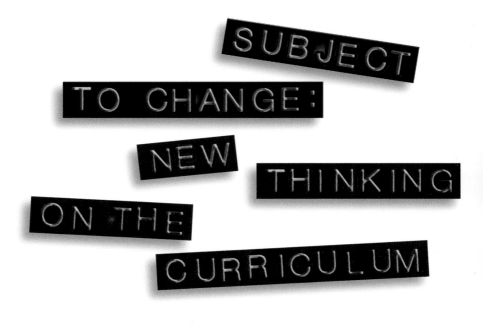

Martin Johnson with contributions from
Nansi Ellis, Alan Gotch, Alison Ryan, Chris
Foster, Julie Gillespie and Monique Lowe

First published in 2007
by the Association of Teachers and lecturers
7 Northumberland Street London WC2N 5RD

Designed and typeset by Peter Coombs

Printed and bound in Great Britain by
The Green Tree Press Ltd, Eastleigh, Hampshire

ISBN 1-902466-58-6

CONTENTS

PREFACE

The curriculum should be treasured

The curriculum should be treasured. There should be real pride in *our* curriculum: it is after all the learning that the nation has decided it should set before its young. Teachers, parents, the wider education community, the employment community, the media and the public at large should all see the curriculum as something that they embrace, support and celebrate. Most of all, young people should relish the opportunity for discovery and achievement that the curriculum offers them.

One problem is that, in this country, the grown-ups argue about the ingredients, the raw materials and the components of the curriculum. Is this river in or out? Do we want this battle or that? Where is my favourite piece of scientific knowledge? Such debate is important. The challenge, therefore, is to blend the curriculum ingredients into something nourishing and appetising.

How can it be made nourishing and appetising? Well, by seeing subject discipline as more vital than subject content, by seeing links between subjects, by seeing the world through important dimensions such as globalisation, technology or sustainability, we start to create a *sense of learning*. By providing a curriculum based on real purpose and real audiences we have a chance of engaging children in compelling experiences that offer a chance for them to understand processes. By assessing progress on a range of measures we will see growth in the individual.

We do it all by viewing the curriculum as a big picture, one that can be explored from different starting points, where organisation of learning follows clearly established decisions about what we want to achieve. Of course, such aims will be different for different communities, though there will be a universal core; there should be a local emphasis within curriculum design but within national parameters. At the Qualifications and Curriculum Authority (QCA) we believe schools want support with curriculum design rather than emphasis on the detail of the content.

This book, *Subject to Change: New thinking on the curriculum*, is a good contribution to the debate. It highlights what the Association of Teachers and Lecturers (ATL) sees as vital professional concerns for all teachers, whether in the union or not. It raises solid argument built upon evidence for decision-makers to consider in their efforts to provide the very best for our children.

The book is a thoughtful read. It puts forward a professional voice, asks searching questions and provides serious argument. It is a positive book, looking for a better future for learning, and in so doing seeks out the treasure of the curriculum.

Mick Waters

Director of Curriculum

Qualification and Curriculum Authority

FOREWORD

The school curriculum goes to the heart of our conception of ourselves as a civil society. We define the values and the aspirations we hold, collectively, through our choices of what to teach our children.

This is why debates about the curriculum are always impassioned, always heated and always difficult. Because the issue is so complex, politicians (who want to keep things simple) have, for too long and far too often, opted for the easy way out; locking the national curriculum into a subject-based mould which was outdated in the nineteenth, never mind the twenty-first century.

The consequences of this approach should be cause for alarm. Young people in Britain walk away from full-time education when they reach young adulthood and they do not return. We are the poor man of the industrially developed nations for staying-on rates post age-16.

The challenge, therefore, is clear: how do we develop a curriculum that will engage the interests, the minds and the aspirations of the current and future generations? To meet this challenge we cannot go down the usual routes of looking forward to a rosy past (the favourite option of the politicians) or meddling round the edges (the favourite option of the civil servants).

ATL, the education union, does not shirk from this key debate, nor does it believe that half measures will do.

Our radical policy on curriculum is powerfully argued and evidenced in this book, authored by Martin Johnson, acting deputy general secretary of ATL and head of education, along with contributions from colleagues in ATL's education department.

Why are we radical? Because we believe that things are *so broke* they cannot be *fixed* by half measures. We need to do things differently, and to do better, if we are to prepare young people for a world in which what is known to be true changes by the hour; a world in which access to information is at the touch of a keyboard, where rote learning of facts must give way to nurturing through education of essential transferable skills that enable the next generation to navigate the information age.

That is why we advocate a skills-based curriculum. One that is focused on communication, physical, interpersonal and intrapersonal skills and thinking and learning skills; all essential components of the educated person able to think and act effectively in the twenty-first century.

Such a curriculum would, of course, develop skills through content, but the subject content of this curriculum, and its organisation, would not be decided by civil servants in Whitehall. It would be designed by teachers, working locally in their communities, to engage the interests and develop the abilities of their pupils.

This approach would accomplish two important things. First it would raise educational standards because we would have classrooms in which pupils were highly engaged, motivated and successful. Second, it would re-professionalise teachers who would be given the authority and responsibility to develop curricula (a key professional skill taken from them by the current centralised approach).

Nor, in this book, do we shirk the issue of assessment. ATL has a long and proud history of opposing the test burden under which we place our children. This burden might be justified if it raised standards of achievement. But it does not. So we argue that national assessment should be delayed until it is needed: at the end of compulsory education at age-16.

Finally, don't make the mistake of dismissing these arguments before you've read this book. Whatever the solution to the problem of the curriculum, we cannot continue with more of the same. We need to radically change our approach to what we teach, how we teach and what, when and how we assess if we are to remain a competitive nation in the globalised economy. There is not much time left, so we need to act now.

Dr Mary Bousted
General secretary, ATL

Introduction

Everyone's talking about it. Lots of people want to change it. Some politicians of the 'must modernise public services' frame of mind refuse to contemplate modernising it. Some teachers shudder at the thought of changing it again.

'It' is the national curriculum. This book is about it. It argues for a fresh start and asks that we go back to first principles, to think through what today's young people need as they pass through the difficult time that apparently is an English childhood and into post-compulsory education. The answers look very different from today's offering, which is based, allegedly, on a conversation between Margaret Thatcher and her hairdresser, and on tradition as experienced by Kenneth Baker, Secretary of State for Education and Science in 1988.

The simple fact that a debate about the curriculum is under way is in itself important in view of the recent politics of education. In England, of course, education has had a high profile ever since Tony Blair uttered the famous education cubed mantra, and the Government has very largely set the agenda by means of continual initiatives, frequent legislation, and an obsession with news management. The paradox behind what appears to be never-ending change is a basic conservatism in Labour's education policy. From 1997, the Government took over Conservative policies and intensified them, arguing 'standards not structures' to justify to its supporters an unexpected inaction over the abolition of academic selection. Without defining, or indeed understanding 'standards'[1] the Government took the occasional brave step to improve the quality of teaching, and focused single-mindedly on English and maths, while promoting the test culture. Pupil performance as *measured* by tests has certainly risen, but there is doubt as to the real underlying improvement in achievement[2].

It wasn't long before the Government gave into the temptation to tinker with secondary school structures in the name of increasing choice, and it has been content to stand on the twin pillars of standards and choice ever since. When it dabbled in the curriculum, it burnt its fingers over the poorly implemented reform of 'A' Levels, and did not apply the leverage necessary for many schools to take seriously its concern with citizenship. The Government recognised the weight of opinion that the offer for 14–19 year-olds was inadequate, but would not back the recommendations of its own enquiry and fell back on a tried, tested and failed vocational solution.

In short, the Labour government has been timid on the curriculum and does not see it as an issue. When it called for a review of how schools might look in 2020 it had 'personalisation' in mind but stated that what would be taught and how it might be assessed was not open for discussion.

The Government is out of step. Schools and educationists see both the curriculum and assessment as very significant issues. Their concerns are many and various. Here are some of them. There is a lack of fit between the widely supported foundation stage and key stage 1. The interference of politicians in the teaching of early reading proves, once again, the truth of the traditional statement regarding 'a little knowledge'. The curriculum as taught in key stage 2 narrows as the all important key stage tests approach. In secondary schools pupils often disengage in key stage 3. Disengagement increases at key stage 4, and although vocational alternatives to the academic curriculum are widely seen as the answer, there are practical problems around such provision. Pupils with special educational needs are disadvantaged at all ages by the current curriculum. And high stakes testing distorts the work of schools, in particular the breadth and balance of the curriculum as taught.

According to a recent survey, less than four percent of teachers believe that the national curriculum meets the needs of all their pupils[3]. Almost 90% of teachers want their school to have greater freedom to develop the curriculum. At the same time, however, many teachers are naturally worried about the possible workload implications of being given greater autonomy over the curriculum.

Teachers in many schools are nonetheless acting on their dissatisfaction. One of the most surprising findings to emerge from research for this book was just how many schools have replaced the national curriculum with their own. Until recently, most of them were keeping resolutely quiet about it, as they were unsure that they should be so innovative. This has occurred mainly in primary schools. Typically, the starting point for them was a sense that their pupils were not learning what they needed to learn. In many cases they then created a framework of the skills their pupils did need and organised their teaching around it, whilst ensuring that their pupils were still prepared for the tests and that the curriculum met with statutory requirements. Such schools often report the outcomes as both improved test results and motivation to learn.

At a time when teachers feel under pressure, the widespread willingness to spend time and effort in creating better learning opportunities shows both the strength of opinion and the high quality of professionalism within the teaching profession and contrasts heavily with the Government's complacency. But their efforts have received a commendation from an unlikely source, the QCA. The statement by Mick Waters, its Head of Curriculum, in the Preface to this book would have seemed extraordinary until recently:

'there should be a local emphasis within curriculum design but within national parameters'.

As good as his word, Mick Waters has led a redesign of key stage 3, intended to give that local flexibility.

Apart from teachers and the QCA, others question whether the present national curriculum and assessment is appropriate. There is increasing academic evidence casting doubt on education system performance, and academics in general are prone to making negative comments about school leavers' preparedness for the self-organised study of higher education. This is attributed to the spoon-feeding approach of teachers trying to squeeze grades from their pupils throughout their school lives.

Other educationists question policy on more philosophical grounds. The recent paper by the philosopher John White[4] suggests that the comprehensive list of aims for the curriculum published in 2000 is essentially a checklist of statements vague enough to satisfy most tastes that schools largely then ignore when planning their work. He suggests we should examine the curriculum closely by questioning the efficacy of each component and how it enables pupils to 'flourish' in the widest sense of the word, not simply in the instrumental and economic senses.

There is also the voice of the employers. It is notoriously difficult to establish what employers in general think about schools. Most have little knowledge of current practice and resort to supporting their own experience as a model. Their representative organisations are inconsistent. However, we ought to pay some attention to the frequently repeated claim that school leavers lack the skills and dispositions required by employers.

From the Government's point of view, all this noise about the weakness of the curriculum would not matter if did not impinge on its education policy priorities. But it does. Despite continued pressure, the ability of schools to force ever higher levels of tested achievement is running out of steam. Results at 11+ have flattened out, with little room for further increases at 16+. However, the central demand for raised standards has been expressed with greater elaboration during Labour's term of office. In recent years the emphasis has been on raising the achievement of those currently least successful. There are two motives for this, highlighted by different elements within the Government. First is the need for the whole workforce to be more capable in the face of global economic competition, an argument that is well over a century old. Second is the importance to social justice of ensuring that every citizen is employable and able to contribute to society whilst enjoying its benefits.

Yet the Organisation for Economic Co-operation and Development's PISA project[5], an international comparative study of attainment in language, maths and science, suggests that of the higher achieving countries England and Wales has the highest *range* of achievement. To date, the evidence is that the gap between the highest and lowest achievers is, if anything, increasing. Despite both intense pressure on and substantial support for secondary schools with large proportions of low achievers, the trickle down approach seems to be unsuccessful.

The relatively low education and training participation rate of seventeen year-olds has also been accepted as another indicator of the need for policy development. The Government's response is to consider making such participation compulsory. There is a very good reason why this proposal has been received with a degree of derision. The 13% of school leavers who decline to stay on fail to be motivated by what's on offer at school and have suffered self-esteem damage through repeated test failure. More of the same will not result in more children staying on and employers are unwilling to offer training at the levels these youngsters need.

The Government is prepared to devote considerable resources to policies to deal with low achievement. They include early years interventions and the whole extended services agenda. However, it is not yet prepared to confront a solution that is staring it in the face. Achievement and post-compulsory participation will rise when pupils are offered throughout their school lives a curriculum that meets their needs and an assessment system that celebrates their successes rather than highlighting their failures.

This does not mean that a new curriculum is needed just for low achievers. This book argues that *all* our pupils are impoverished by the current offering. Attitudes to the learning of the successful are just as problematic as the disengagement of the unsuccessful. This book aims to add to the noise about the curriculum, to increase the pressure on the Government to turn its attention to it in a progressive way, and to pave the way to a time when all the nation's pupils can look forward to school days with the prospect of meaningful learning experiences.

During 2006 the volume of debate on these issues increased dramatically. In part this was stimulated by the

2020 Review and in part it was due to discussions about the value of the secondary curriculum development, which is being sponsored by the Government. Mainly it was due to the growing realisation that schools have gone as far as they can within the present policy envelope.

We need to spell out some boundaries to the discussion. The first is geographical. Some of the arguments deployed in the following chapters have universal application, some less so, and some apply only to England. Although we show how the other governments of the UK are addressing the same issues, the main focus is England and England's national curriculum.

The second boundary is the age range to be included. This is a much less simple question. The compulsory years of schooling are from age five to age 16, but there are good reasons for considering a longer time span.

One result of the Government's emphasis on improving opportunities in the early years has been considerable curriculum development, including the Early Years Foundation Stage. From 2008 it will become part of the national curriculum, although only parts will be statutory. It is not organised on a subject basis, used by other parts of the national curriculum; instead it takes a much more holistic view to the development of the child and their consequential learning needs. Indeed, the proper way to develop the new curriculum, and advocated here, would be to start from the early years and to build the expected skills framework as a chronological progression. However, while England remains one of a minority of countries that compels school attendance from age five, there is logic in a statutory curriculum starting from that age, and this book takes that approach. One of the improvements that would result from this would be the seamless transition between the foundation stage and the rest of the national curriculum.

At the other end of the age range, the 16+ boundary seems problematic for two reasons. The first is the proposal to raise the age of compulsory participation. The second is altogether more substantial, the development of 14–19 as a distinct stage. But although this label has been widely accepted, in practice there are few signs of the development of a coherent progression through this age. Even schools with sixth-forms continue to regard the GCSE as a break; for many pupils, post-16 means a change of institution. For many, there is a lack of appropriate post-16 courses. In a quasi-market, competition for students limits co-ordinated planning of learners' progression. Another reason for regarding 16+ as a break is that there is a compelling case for a national system of pupil assessment at school leaving age. In view of all this, this book does not regard 14–19 as a stage but believes the national curriculum should apply to the end of compulsory education and makes proposals for the curriculum for age five-16. The proposals will have significant knock-on effects on post-compulsory curriculum, but that's an issue for another time.

This book is based on the *Subject to Change* policy adopted by ATL's Executive Committee in 2006. ATL believes that education staff are professionals who care about both pay and conditions of service and also about wider education and professional issues. Teachers have the understanding and the authority to speak knowledgeably about policy and practice, about the purposes of education and about social justice, and have a responsibility to debate the issues locally and nationally. What teachers are asked to teach is a key issue for a teachers' union to debate.

ATL' s longstanding policy has the following elements:

- All children and young people should be entitled to a curriculum that is broad, balanced and relevant to their learning needs and not only on training for the world of work.

- There should be greater coherence in the principles and values across the key stages and consistency with the foundation stage.

- Debate on the curriculum should involve the widest possible variety of people with an interest, including school staff, parents, pupils, school governors, researchers and academics, as well politicians.

- The principle of subsidiarity should apply to the school curriculum; decisions should be made at the lowest appropriate level.

- The QCA and its equivalents in Scotland, Wales and Northern Ireland should ensure curriculum manageability in a variety of school contexts.

- Any change to the school curriculum should be properly costed, trialled and evaluated before it is implemented.

ATL's *Teaching to Learn* campaign, culminating in a conference in 2005, developed a critique of current policy on the curriculum and assessment. With *Subject to Change*, ATL went on to develop positive proposals for an alternative way. These proposals still remain controversial amongst some ATL members, but the lead offered by its Executive enables a contribution to the wider debate.

The next chapter sets the scene by discussing some of the ways the curriculum has been envisioned. It makes the point that in our society knowledge is socially organised; some knowledge has higher status and this affects government decisions on what ought to be taught and decisions by learners on the relevance of schooling.

We then take a look at the recent history of curriculum development in England, and in particular the national curriculum. Chapter four discusses in detail the proposal to redesign the national curriculum by defining the skills required by tomorrow's citizens, and chapter five goes on to consider the place of knowledge in the curriculum.

Chapter six looks at the implications of these proposals for pupil assessment. Chapter seven provides some comfort, perhaps, for those teachers mentioned earlier who shudder at the thought of more change and more work. Chapter seven suggests that teachers have lots to gain and little to lose from a new kind of curriculum and assessment system.

We know there is already a lot of published material on the weaknesses of the present system. It is clear that this book starts from the assumptions that many of the arguments in this critique are justified and that the majority of teachers agree.

But that is no longer enough. When even the Government's own agency for the curriculum is trying to encourage new ways of thinking about the curriculum, it is time for the debate to move on. All of us committed to the best possible education for our young people have a responsibility now to be positive. In saying that the national curriculum needs a substantial overhaul we all have to go on to say what a new national curriculum should look like.

This book tries to achieve this. We know it will produce strong reactions, both of support and of outrage. A more detailed debate about the future curriculum must now take place, and this book is a contribution. If, as we believe, the Government will eventually concede that change is necessary, educationists, including teachers, must have contributed their ideas. This is the moment when the hackneyed clause applies: no change is not an option.

References

1 Richards, C. 2005. *Standards in English primary schools: are they rising?* ATL, London.

2 Tymms, P. 2004. *Are standards rising in British primary schools?* British Education Research Journal, 30: 477–94.

3 ATL. 2006. Online survey of teacher opinion, September 2006.

4 White, J. (2007) *What are schools are for and why?* IMPACT, number 14. Philosophy of Education Society of Great Britain, Staffordshire.

5 Organisation for Economic Co-operation and Development. 2001. *Knowledge and skills for life: first results*. OECD, Paris, and Organisation for Economic Co-operation and Development. 2004. *Learning for tomorrow's world: first results*. OECD, Paris.

CHAPTER TWO

Thinking about the curriculum

Anyone who has had a fiver for every book ever written about the curriculum would be a wealthy person. This would be especially true if we were to start with Plato and the principles behind the Academy he established in approximately 387BC. Incidentally, there is no record of the Athenian government providing huge sums for Plato to set up the Academy with him providing just a pittance. If we stick with contemporary items on the subject, there are 4,936 in the London Institute of Education library. Readers anticipating a learned treatise on the history of thought and what ought to be passed on from generation to generation should look there not here. However, it is necessary to touch in passing some of this 'thought' in order to provide a background for the proposals for a new curriculum for England that follow in later chapters. To begin with it would be helpful to clarify what is meant by the curriculum.

'A curriculum is a blueprint for what we want children to become'.

Mike Newby, Emeritus Professor of Education at Plymouth University and advocate for curriculum development.

Another simple (at least on the surface) definition is in answer to the question, 'what should children learn?' Curriculum content can be set out in terms of outcomes (what should a child know, understand or be able to do) and processes or learning experiences. Content can be based around knowledge, as subjects or areas of learning, skills and competencies, dispositions and feelings[1].

One aspect of the definition used here is that it includes only *planned* learning experiences. It has long been understood that in school children learn many things both inside and outside lessons that were not intended. This was known as 'the hidden curriculum'. Mick Waters, from the QCA, points out that children learn useful lessons in a variety of ways outside school and encourages schools to incorporate recognition of this type of learning. It may well be important for schools to be conscious of this, but a definition of curriculum limited to intended learning outcomes is more workable for our purposes. The school curriculum is intended to comprise all learning and other experiences planned by the school for its pupils.

Many philosophers have started at the highest level of generality with an aim. Historically, this aim has often taken the form of a description of the educated man, or the 'good man'. This approach is hardly surprising since the predominant pattern of education through the ages has been the one-to-one tutoring of the wealthy. The aim was to produce an accomplished young man who could use his adult leisure and power wisely. With the great intellectual movements of the Renaissance and the Enlightenment in Europe, wider perspectives were applied to the aims of education. Then, in nineteenth century Britain, as school became more popular amongst the privileged classes, the aim of producing a class capable of ruling an empire became more manifest; Thomas Arnold introduced mathematics, modern history and modern languages to Rugby School.

In the last century western philosophers have continued to ponder the aims of education in very different social circumstances as modern societies moved towards mass or universal state education. However, this very process led to a substantial widening of the debate. When a state takes responsibility for educating its people, the aims of education become a political as well as a philosophical question, and when that state endorses an open society the political debate becomes a popular debate. As the twentieth century progressed some states took their responsibility seriously enough to stipulate the curriculum in their schools with varying degrees of rigidity. For obvious reasons, totalitarian states are more likely to impose a detailed curriculum, but they are not alone.

So, however much the thinkers of a particular age may assume their statements have universal application, we find that they are constrained by the economic, social and political circumstances of their times; thus the taken-for-granted education in one age became the history of another. In the past, for example, it was assumed that boys and girls required different kinds of education, in view of their heavily segregated adult roles. Only recently in western societies have education systems moved some way towards eradicating gendered education[2].

Even more pertinent to the argument in this book, much curriculum thinking in an era of mass education assumes different provision for different social classes, or for those who will occupy different economic roles (which amounts to the same thing), or at least for those of different dispositions (which also amounts to the same thing). A major basis for the proposals to follow is that in the twenty-first century we need a comprehensive curriculum for a comprehensive era; that throughout compulsory schooling there are some learning experiences needed by all.

Whatever the aims and objectives of education described by philosophers, until the last century detailed taxonomies were set out in the form of subjects. Although each subject had its own methods and skills, it was described predominantly in terms of its knowledge. Facts were considered non-problematic. Take history, it was considered to be important to learn what had happened and when but not to question how we came to know these things.

It is hardly surprising that in an age where education was the property of the privileged, the subjects thought worthy of inclusion in a curriculum were intellectual. With the exception of the arts, which required technical skill, the proper activity of education was considered to be thought. When nineteenth century British public schools expanded their curricula they did not go beyond 'academic subjects'.

However, at the same time the churches were developing education for the masses. Responding to the needs of the new urban poor they offered godliness, Christian morality, tidy personal habits, the ability to read the scriptures and basic arithmetic. English pragmatism took precedence over grand philosophy. The practical superseded the intellectual.

It is almost axiomatic that governments are comprised largely of people who have been academically successful, and who tend to support the kind of education practised by their own schools and universities. It is not surprising that when state education was introduced, the organising principle adopted for the secondary curriculum was the subject. In England, the subjects adopted were English language and literature, maths, science, history, geography, a language, physical exercise, drawing, singing, manual training and housewifery for girls. This list does include a small practical element, but since only a minority of the working class attended secondary school at this time this was probably unnecessary. As the next chapter describes, a slightly updated version of the above list was adopted for the national curriculum in a very different era.

There are many ways other than the familiar knowledge/ subjects in which to design a curriculum. In 1931, a report of the Hadow Committee stated that 'the curriculum is to be thought of in terms of activity and experience rather than of knowledge to be acquired and facts to be stored'. Today this looks like a modern and challenging statement, although it went on to describe the curriculum in terms of subjects. It is in line with current theories of learning which it predates. These are considered below.

A more common development was to move to what is known as cross-curricular taxonomies of the traditional subjects. In the 1960s, Schwab suggested three disciplines (investigative, appreciative and decisive)[3], while Peterson suggested modes of thinking and experience (logical, empirical, moral and aesthetic). In 1970 Hirst and Peters suggested areas of knowledge: human studies, philosophy, moral judgement and awareness, religious understanding, formal logic and mathematics, physical sciences and aesthetic experience[4]. This approach continues to assume that education is almost entirely about intellectual development. It seeks to find common elements across subject boundaries. For our purposes there are two noteworthy implications of this line of work.

Firstly, by picking up the idea of curriculum as 'experience', they confirmed the importance of process as well as defining outcome. Secondly, they confirmed that 'the subject' is not in any sense a logical necessity; an objective reality outside human creation. The subject is a convenient category, one way of organising knowledge.

A further step in rethinking the curriculum was taken by Her Majesty's Inspectors of Schools (HMI), in a period when they were an independent elite cadre of the teaching profession. In 1977 HMI suggested eight areas of experience: the aesthetic and creative; the ethical; the linguistic; the mathematical; the physical; the scientific; the social and political and the spiritual[5]. The significance of this typology is the movement away from an exclusively intellectual experience. By promoting creativity, the physical, and social and political experience, HMI embraced a more rounded view of the learning needs of children.

Considering the curriculum by analysing children's needs is another twentieth century development, perhaps related to changes in their social status. In England this is reflected particularly in curriculum statements for early years education. Instead of starting with the 'good man' the question becomes, what makes a 'good' childhood? What do we know about how children learn? What do children need in order to learn?

A sophisticated curriculum adopting this approach is Te Whàriki early years curriculum from New Zealand. Te Whàriki is woven from four principles and from five essential areas of learning and development and focuses on the child and their relationships. It implicitly encourages learning with the promotion of cultural and community values.

Two theories of child development in particular have influenced both the curriculum and teachers in Britain. In the 1920s Jean Piaget suggested that children go through a series of age-related stages in the development of their thinking and were unable to understand particular concepts until they reached a particular stage.

Piaget also proposed the theory of 'equilibration', whereby children's thinking developed through a process of accommodation and assimilation. In many instances, children assimilate new knowledge into their 'world view', but when a new piece of knowledge will not fit into this 'world view', they will need to change the structure of their thinking in order to accommodate the new knowledge. Hence, offering experiences which are relevant to children's needs and interests and offering them in a relevant context is important if teachers are not to swamp children with new knowledge that they are unable to accommodate.

Piaget's image of the child was of an individual learner as a 'lone scientist'. For Vygotsky, learning was a social activity, whereby the child learns in playful interaction with others, be they adults or children. He defined three zones of development: the zone of actual development, where a child shows what they can do alone and independently; the zone of proximal or potential development, where a child shows what they can only do with help; and the zone of future development, which is what the child will be able to do later. The importance of the zone of proximal development is in showing the importance of the teacher's role in supporting or 'scaffolding' children's learning. This is not merely about letting children explore what interests them, but about providing manageable challenge to move them on in their thinking. Relationships and social development are important for learning, but learning is still centred around the child rather than around notions of adult-imposed goals to be achieved.

Recent research into brain function has provided some insight into the ways in which children learn, although there is disagreement about how much we can use the findings to support theories of learning. A child's brain, up to approximately the age of ten, has more synapses than at any other time of life. Others have argued that attitudes to learning are embedded as early as age six[6]. Children need a variety of experiences so that connections can form in their brains. These experiences preferably need to be multi-sensory, since learning is multi faceted and practical, since neural pathways are formed through repeated use.

The theory that children learn best when they are interdependent, challenged in their zone of proximal development, and when they are able to develop their own theories about the world around them, is likely to result in a different curriculum (and in particular a different form of pedagogy) from a theory that suggests that there are particular and age-related stages through which children pass. The current national curriculum is more of a reflection of the latter than the former.

The curriculum proposals which follow assume that the best learning is social and active, with opportunities to make decisions and errors. Learning is more likely to be long-lasting if children have opportunities to become engrossed and are challenged at the edges of their capabilities. In this view, the curriculum is described in terms of a process as well as intended outcomes; the habits of learning are just as important as the items learnt.

Indeed, more advanced versions of this line stress that children create knowledge. As the action research project Enquiring Minds[7] puts it:

'children are active agents in social life; they construct meaning out of their diverse experiences. Though this may sound obvious, it is important to realise that this is not the view on which much schooling is based'.

Now it is true that a pedagogy which responds to, rather than imposing on, the learner, is not impossible within current curriculum arrangements. Research from ATL demonstrates that the most effective teachers are those who are able to create a classroom dynamic in which pupils develop a sense of ownership[8]. This is very difficult to achieve, however, when the knowledge content to be covered is so tightly prescribed. This work also confirms how much the present regime is resented by pupils.

The idea of the learner as agent, who puts together their own discoveries to create their own knowledge, does not lead necessarily to a proposal for pupil control of the curriculum. What is necessary is flexibility; a recognition that learning outcomes, in terms of knowledge certainly, are unpredictable. The ever increasing trend, sponsored by the Government, to focus on the learning side of the teaching and learning mantra itself leads inexorably away from a model of the pupil as an empty vessel towards a model of the pupil as an active social being who creates their own understanding.

In the second half of the twentieth century, then, there was increasing debate across two dimensions of the curriculum. One was the question of what children ought to be learning and the other was who should decide, especially whether the state should make at least some of these decisions.

This debate ignored other discourses about the curriculum and the question of who was to control it. Long before 1988, the sociologist MFD Young[9] pointed out that definitions of what counts as knowledge are problematic and reflect power relations in society. Around the same time, the historian Richard Johnson used the phrase 'really useful knowledge' to describe the content of self-help adult education amongst politically radical groups in the early 1800s. These groups rejected the content of 'provided' education and valued political and economic studies, as well as husbandry and some natural science. So the question of what constitutes really useful knowledge may be answered differently by different groups within society.

At one level, it would appear that prior to 1988 the curriculum in England's schools was under the sole control of teachers. Even the design of exam syllabuses, which constrained the upper secondary years, was undertaken by exam boards with overwhelming teacher representation. Sociologists of knowledge would ask, however, about the cultural influences on these decision makers, who were largely the products of schools and universities strongly based on subject-organised and largely positivistic concepts of knowledge. This way of thinking had, and has, high status due to its association with the values of the privileged classes. The concept of the subject is deeply embedded in this culture and associated institutions, including crucially traditional universities. This makes it plausible that support for a subject-organised curriculum is taken-for-granted, as referred to earlier, with all this implies for the difficulties in gaining acceptance for alternatives.

On the other hand, the inheritors of the elementary school tradition of meeting the practical needs of the working classes, in some cases extended into a commitment to 'really useful knowledge', occupy a minority alternative position which leads to a continuing debate amongst educationists. In the case of primary practitioners, the emphasis on the needs of the whole child leads away from a subject organisation. In the case of higher education, more vocationally-oriented universities offer cross-curricular degrees.

This discussion highlights an important characteristic of thinking about the curriculum: what children ought to learn is a political decision. What you want youngsters to learn depends on your view of the purpose of education, and that depends on your view of the nature of society. Much recent debate avoids dealing explicitly with this inevitability but the issues do not go away. In this book we confront a major political question: is it right to design a curriculum for compulsory school years which effectively provides differentiation on class lines? It was taken for granted in Britain for many years but whilst it remains the case in a comprehensive era it somehow doesn't seem right.

The political question, 'who should control the curriculum?' has been settled in Britain and elsewhere by the introduction of a national curriculum. The argument goes that education is too important to be left to the educators, the state has a duty to decide. In England, an ideologically anti–state government in the 1980s accepted the consensus that state compulsion was necessary because educators had failed to provide what society apparently expected: a broad and balanced curriculum for all.

The idea that all pupils should have a guaranteed entitlement to such an offer was attractive to a wide range of people. In modern society it is widely accepted that the state has the right and the responsibility to underwrite this kind of guarantee. In itself, however, this does not dictate how the entitlement is to be defined. In the next chapter we demonstrate how the English national curriculum came to be a highly detailed full-coverage monster but here reflect that this is not the only possible model.

Breadth and balance could be guaranteed by means of a very general specification; a requirement to teach a list of subjects, or areas of experience, would be sufficient in itself. This model is operated in some other countries. A state which demands greater control could add sub-headings, perhaps. However, that level of generality does not allow for a standardised assessment system. There is no necessary connection between a national curriculum and national testing, but in England the two came together because the legislation introducing the curriculum also introduced tests as accountability and market information mechanisms. Curriculum designers know that this is how not to do it, assessment should follow curriculum, but in England the 'core' subjects were described in sufficient detail to be the syllabuses for a series of national tests: curriculum following assessment. When the curriculum is subordinate to the test there is inevitably an undue emphasis on knowledge outcomes rather than the learning process with consequent damage to pupils' overall experience.

Apart from level of detail, another open question is the coverage of a national curriculum. This has two dimensions.

Firstly, what proportion of the learning programme should it cover? How much of the school week should be determined by the state? This question has never been settled in England. As we shall see, the original version of the national curriculum was so large that it would have occupied far more than 100% of the time available, and although a review aimed to bring the figure down to 80% in practice most schools assume that it is the whole curriculum. Again, there is no necessary reason why state prescription should be total; other countries leave space for local determination.

Secondly, what age groups should be covered by this entitlement? There is a strong argument for it to cover all of compulsory education, and this is the position adopted in this book. However, there is currently in England an uncomfortable boundary between the early years curriculum and key stage 1, this issue would be resolved by means of our proposals for the national curriculum.

At the other end of the age range there must be some doubt as to the present state of entitlement to breadth and balance. Since the standard academic offer has always been unattractive to a proportion of pupils it can hardly have been a surprise that the original academic national curriculum key stage 4 led to bottom up pressure for alternatives. And since the generally accepted alternative was a derivation of the 'practically useful' elementary school offer, it is also unsurprising that what is now termed as 'vocational pathways' should have been seen as appropriate. The outcome was to maintain a differentiated curriculum for older pupils that does not secure breadth and balance for all. Our proposals resolve this issue as well.

So the concept of a universal entitlement underwritten by the state continues to be appropriate. What needs rethinking is the current English interpretation, which provides a complete coverage with required knowledge defined in fine detail. But a curriculum is also about skills, attitudes and dispositions.

The OECD suggests that we live in a 'knowledge economy' but we need to think carefully about what actually constitutes knowledge. It proposes four distinct types, know-what, know-why, know-how and know-who, and suggests that there is growing demand for the latter three compared with the more straightforward factual knowledge embodied in know-what[10]. The traditional school curriculum is certainly of the know-what category, but know-why is possibly what is described later as deep learning, in which connections are made between items of knowledge so that the learner develops understanding.

This formulation suggests that what school-leavers can do is more important than what they know. In Chapter 4 we discuss why it is appropriate to organise a national curriculum in terms of skills clearly related to know-how. Every subject has specific skills associated with it. These have not always been made explicit in the curriculum. Increasingly, however, curriculum thinkers have become concerned with other types of skills not directly related to subject disciplines that are more generic. Whether to include these in a national curriculum, and if so how, is another debate which marks out the divide between supporters of academic and practical curricula.

The debate is confused, not least because of knee-jerk interventions from government in response to evidence of gaps in the coverage of the national curriculum. For example, the Government decided that 'key skills': application of number, IT, communication, problem solving, working with others and improving own learning and performance, should be taught across the curriculum. These should not be confused with the 'basic skills' of literacy, numeracy and ICT. More recently the QCA has devised a framework of personal, learning and thinking skills. They comprise six areas and suggest that pupils should be 'independent enquirers', 'creative thinkers', 'reflective learners', 'team workers', 'self-managers' and 'effective participators'. Actually, these are not descriptors of skills but of human characteristics associated with more specific skills. They go beyond a subject-based curriculum and in fact clash with it.

In England, such lists of skills are added to the national curriculum. They are not integrated, they do not have the same statutory basis, and they are not explicitly assessed. The QCA recommends that schools should map the skills onto existing subject programmes of study. This can be done, and has already been done in pioneering schools across the country. Nevertheless, this is not a smart way to design a curriculum, and certainly does not create coherence.

Bealings Primary School, Suffolk

At Bealings Primary School the headteacher was inspired to revamp the curriculum and introduced *REAL* (Realistic Experience for Active Learning). Using extended role-play exercises, pupils are able to develop more realistic skills; the entire national curriculum is taught through this means. The curriculum is brought to life as pupils engage in fictional scenarios where they can act at being 'experts' working for a company. Teachers continue with a project for as long as they feel the children are engaged and challenged. The children are able to build skills in teamwork, communication, independent learning and problem solving. Teachers at Bealings Primary believe that allowing the children to become 'experts' not only motivates them to learn but also dramatically changes the way they learn. Staff ensure that learning matches the national curriculum, however, the school feels that they have the freedom to teach it in a unique way. Children enjoy this way of learning and gain a better sense of reality, demonstrating confidence well beyond their years.

The curriculum should encourage the development of skills within a framework that shapes children's dispositions and attitudes. These would probably include such qualities as curiosity, concern, respect, responsibility and the will to act, to achieve and to do what is right as well as commitment to truth, honesty, trust and a sense of justice. A historical vision of a 'good' citizen might include the idea that citizens should question and challenge, should be open-minded, flexible and willing to change; others may view citizenship as being law-abiding and loyal.

Other countries in the UK have made more progress down this path. In a review of the Welsh Curriculum 2000, the Qualifications Curriculum and Assessment Authority for Wales (ACCAC) found an over-emphasis on knowledge and content and an under-emphasis on skills. It recommended the re-organisation and reduction of the programmes of study to enable schools to provide an inclusive coherent curriculum by making links between subjects and making skills more prominent. ACCAC also recommended the Welsh Assembly Government consider, as a long-term goal, the vision of a radically revised curriculum that is more overtly learner-centred and skills-focused and not necessarily subject based. In welcome recognition of the connection between assessment and curriculum the Government decided to introduce teacher assessment of communication, number, and thinking skills to replace key stage 2 tests.

In Scotland, a new 'curriculum for excellence' for children from age 3–18 comes into effect in 2008. In primary schools there will be some adjustment to the curriculum and substantial simplification, with an end to recommended time allocations for each subject area. In secondary schools, it has not broken away from the subject base or the division between academic and vocational, and expects a range of cross-curricular experiences to be bolted on.

Govan High School, Glasgow

Staff at Govan High School realised that pupils needed more skills to enhance their employability than were provided by the standard curriculum. They devised a skills list organised into seven families, and as a whole staff mapped them onto existing schemes of work in the subject organised curriculum. Now subject teachers, and other professionals, focus on the skills in their teaching and informally assess their acquisition. Although still in its early days, staff hope the skills focus will lead to improvements in self-esteem, motivation, and exam performance as well as the more specific skills needed for employment.

In Northern Ireland, the Council for the Curriculum Examinations and Assessment is developing a secondary school curriculum with more emphasis on thinking skills, problem solving and information handling, as well as requiring the inclusion of personal, social and health education, citizenship and employability. At key stage 3 tests will be replaced by a Pupil Profile. At key stage 4 there will be an entitlement framework, which guarantees a minimum of 24 courses on offer; at least one third must be general and one third applied, or vocational.

The conclusions to be drawn from this brief perusal of the curriculum are as follows. The classical and elite model containing a narrow range of intellectual knowledge and skill is inappropriate for an age of universal education. In Britain, this model, with its organisation based on the academic subject, continues to be in competition with models built on the needs of children. Although there has recently been a greater recognition of the importance of developing a wider range of skills, attempts to integrate them into the subject-based curriculum has had limited success.

It is time to make a fresh start. If a curriculum is to centre on the whole range of skills needed by tomorrows' citizens, it must be designed that way from the start. The rest of this book contains proposals for doing this. But first, it may be instructive to take a closer look at how we got to where we are. The next chapter is a brief history of the gestation, birth, and stunted growth of England's national curriculum.

References

1 Katz, L.G. 1998. *A developmental approach to the curriculum in the early years*. In Smidt, S. *The Early Years: A Reader*. London, Routledge.

2 Claire, H. 2004 *Gender in education 3-19: A fresh approach*. London, ATL.

3 Schwab, J. 1962. *The Teaching of Science*. Cambridge, MA, Harvard University Press.

4 Hirst, P. H. and Peters, R. S. 1970. *The Logic of Education*. London, Routledge and Kegan Paul.

5 Her Majesty's Inspectorate. 1977. *Curriculum 11–16*. London, Her Majesty's Stationary Office.

6 Donaldson, M., Grieve, R and Pratt, C. [Eds.] 1983. *Early childhood development and education: reading in psychology*. Oxford, Blackwell.

7 Enquiring Minds Project. *Enquiring Minds: Context and Rationale*. Available online from: http://www.enquiringminds.org.uk/download/pdfs/Enquiring_Minds_context_paper.pdf

8 ATL. 2004. *It's like mixing colours: how young people view their learning within the context of the Key Stage 3 National Strategy*. London, ATL.

9 Young, M. F. D. Year. *Knowledge and Control*. London; Routledge with Open University Press.

10 OECD. 2001. *What Schools for the future?* Paris, OECD

CHAPTER THREE

Where are we now: 1976 and all that

The reader may well wonder why we're choosing to dedicate space in a book on one of the most burning issues of the day in education by looking backwards? The short answer is that a young teacher starting work in 2007 would never have known a time when the school curriculum was not a tightly regulated, centrally imposed 'given'. Their experience, from their own schooldays to their very first foray into the classroom as a fledgling professional, would have been in the context of a nationally determined and prescriptive curriculum. Today content and teaching methods are available to look-up in a loose-leaf folder or on the web; the National Strategies are also available if one still feels the need for guidance and support. It is important to remember how we got to this point. This book is a both critique of the present and a glimpse of a possible future alternative but to achieve this we must understand clearly how we got here.

A history of the school curriculum in state maintained schools could usefully begin as far back as the 1870 Education Act or the 1862 Revised Code. But for our purposes we shall begin in the 1950s when the nation's schools were perceived to be run exclusively by, and some would say for, teachers and their professional collaborators. What were the forces of change that arrived with rock n' roll and television that forced serious consideration of what had been taught in elementary and grammar schools from the nineteenth Century until 1944?

Schools in the 1950s were shaped by the 1944 Education Act, which brought in secondary education for all and a tripartite system of schooling to cater for all abilities and aptitudes. It was widely accepted that there were innate differences between children, which would require distinct modes of schooling. However, the Act was almost silent on the curriculum, implicitly accepting the status quo elitism with its concern largely for the 'clever' child. The exception was the requirement on all schools to teach Religious Education, one component of the settlement of the dispute between Church and state over control of schools, which was a feature of the Act.

Grammar schools, which were left untouched by the Act, were free to continue to offer an 'academic' curriculum, and soon a new exam, the General Certificate of Education (Ordinary Level). The Ordinary ('O') Level for 16 year-olds was awarded for each subject, and replaced the School Certificate, which required a pass in a range of subjects. The 'O' Level was aimed squarely at the top 20% or so of the ability range. Technical schools were an attempt to provide a halfway house between the academic and the non-academic, with the vague perception that these pupils would benefit from a more vocational, but still largely academic, education. Technical schools were established in only a few areas, often becoming *de facto* the grammar school of second choice. And finally, and entering through the tradesman's entrance, came the secondary modern school.

The curriculum difference between grammar and secondary modern schools was mainly one of balance. Grammar schools offered some art and craft more so for their lower streams, whilst secondary modern schools offered more art and craft but did so without neglecting the core subjects and the humanities. The main difference was in assessment. Most grammar school pupils took 'O' Levels, along with some pupils from ambitious secondary modern schools.

The rest took nothing, except for commercial certificates for the office-girls-to-be.

It gradually became apparent to many that this system represented a huge waste of talent and, in a developing egalitarian and optimistic atmosphere, was just plain wrong; all should have the same chance in education and it should not be blighted by a premature sorting of sheep and goats based on selective tests of contestable worth.

Then, in 1957 the launching of Sputnik 1 by the USSR threw the West into a panic. In the late 1950s and early 1960s the UK and the USA both believed the USSR to be stealing a march on them technologically. Questions began to be asked of the suitability of the school curriculum for a technologically advanced society. In 1959 the Crowther Report[1] confirmed what was already known about the effect of social background on educational attainment and lamented the "neglected educational territory" of those who left school at age 15 to follow a craft or technical career.

Thus the comprehensive ideal, appearing in the early 1950s, gradually gained pace. By the end of the 1970s, 81% of English pupils and 96% of those in Wales were in comprehensive schools. The 11+ had virtually disappeared from most of the country[2]. The comprehensive debate also gave rise to the question, 'would a fairer society have a more comprehensive curriculum and assessment system?'

In the fifties, the only constraint on teachers and what they taught was the external examination system. Primary schools still sat the 11+, in many schools taken by a selection of pupils rather than all. And a small proportion of secondary school pupils sat an exam at 16+; most left school at age 15 (the leaving age was not raised to 16 until 1973). There was little sense across the system that teachers should strive to increase the proportion of pupils who were successful in exams. Indeed, as the percentage pass rate of exams was fixed in advance, and as standards might vary from year to year, this was more or less impossible. The culture of pressure to achieve was weak in comparison with the present.

In terms of the curriculum offer, teachers could teach what they liked to the large proportion of pupils who would never sit an exam. Even for those teaching exam syllabuses, there was nothing like the mono-maniacal attention to the exam which is the norm today. If a teacher felt constrained it would have been from the poverty of teaching resources available and not from interference from outside the classroom.

But the fifties were characterised by the beginning of economic and social change, which has only gathered in pace since. One change was the decline of deference, and with that came a wider questioning of the authority of the professional. As the twentieth century progressed the necessity of accountability of the professions, especially those in public services, became ever more urgent. It was inevitable that the question would be raised: is it right for teachers to decide what should be taught?

At first, most educationists continued to argue that this was an area of professional expertise that should be left to them. And most educationists, whatever their philosophical starting point, came up with a preferred curriculum that looked amazingly similar to the status quo; one that was described in terms of knowledge categorised into subjects. But then, in 1960, the Government produced a historic shift of position; for the first time for over half a century it signalled an interest in the curriculum. Criticising the way schools controlled the curriculum as a 'secret garden', David Eccles, the Minister of the time, told Parliament he would make the ministry's voice heard more often and positively, and no doubt controversially[3]. Two years later, in an attempt to exert more control, he established the

Curriculum Study Group (CSG), which was constituted from inspectors and administrators. In 1964 the CSG became the Schools Council for Curriculum and Examinations, which came under the control of representatives of the teacher unions.

The Newsom Report, *Half our future*[4], looked at improving the curriculum for the less academically inclined, and suggested, amongst other things, internal certification. What actually transpired was the Certificate of Secondary Education, the CSE. The CSE was designed for the 80% of pupils who were deemed unable to take 'O' Levels. Typically, this qualification combined final examinations with coursework. The Mode 3 CSE allowed individual teachers to write the syllabus and set the exam, with moderation by the exam board, and this was enthusiastically embraced by many teachers. Unfortunately, and probably inevitably, it became indelibly linked with the secondary modern school and therefore very much perceived as a second-class qualification, despite the equivalence between its highest grade and an 'O' Level pass.

The 1960s primary school is characterised in some quarters as a fun loving free for all where learning took second place to the immediate interests and whims of each individual child. However, as the 11+ declined, there were exciting curriculum developments in some places. Subject barriers were broken down with the development of topic work, which attracted a good deal of interest from the USA as examples of outstanding practice[2].

The use of more progressive methods of teaching in primary schools was given some validation by the *Plowden Report: Children and their primary schools*[5], which has since been made almost synonymous with child centred-education in this country. It drew heavily on the Piaget's notion of child development through certain definite and sequential stages. Children were not to be forced through a curricular mangle but encouraged to take a delight in learning for its own sake and experience the excitement of discovering things for themselves. Emphasis was laid upon the use of assessment in order to plan children's learning appropriately.

'One of the main educational tasks of the primary school is to build on and strengthen the children's intrinsic interest in learning and lead them to learn for themselves rather than from fear or disapproval or desire for praise'.

Central Advisory Council for Education.

A conservative counter-attack over the so called 'discovery' approach, which was perceived to dominate practice in primary schools, began at the end of the 1960s and was given its most eloquent voice through the efforts of the group of commentators who authored the *Black Papers*. The *Black Papers* were a series of articles first published in 1969, which rejected 'progressive' methods in education and called for a return to the traditional grammar school ethos and methods; their spiritual descendents can be found now in the Campaign for Real Education. They were also disparaging of standards generally, and of the level of discipline in comprehensive schools.

But the reality did not match the hype in many schools. When HMI reported on primary practice in 1978[6] they found a continuing stress on basic subjects, with three-quarters of teachers adopting a mainly didactic approach and only five per cent an exploratory approach. By then the 11+ had disappeared from most primary schools but the lack of curriculum breadth and variety remained an issue. The HMI's real concern was over poor work in areas of the curriculum other than the basics: subjects such as science, history and geography were sometimes under-resourced, poorly taught or given insufficient time (a criticism which still resonates in OfSTED reports of primary practice). The evidence is that schools had 'outline syllabuses' in mathematics and English, and sometimes other subjects, but, there was little rigorous assessment of achievement and as a consequence little opportunity for the monitoring of individual progress or planning future work on the basis of achievement[7].

Similar evidence accumulated with respect to secondary schools. A pupil's opportunity to experience a balanced curriculum depended on variables such as their location, school type and categorised ability; all of which remained closely linked with social class and particularly gender. The genderised curriculum remains a problem to-date but was much more obvious, and usually unquestioned, until the curriculum debate got under way.

As the sixties turned into the seventies, education remained a low profile political issue, dominated by the comprehensive debate and enlivened only by accusations of milk-snatching. Questions of the curriculum continued to be seen as professional issues, despite the efforts of the *Black Paper*ites and an associated public unease with 'standards'.

Then, on the 18 October 1976, Prime Minister James Callaghan delivered a speech at Ruskin college, Oxford, which laid the groundwork for reforms in the 1980s involving taking responsibility for the curriculum away from teachers in the classroom and giving it to central government. For the first time in public a need for a 'core curriculum' was described. Callaghan also addressed what he regarded as education's failure to respond to the demands of industry: a recurring theme before and since the Ruskin speech. Callaghan professed that the 'secret garden' should be opened up for government and public inspection.

'I would say that we must carry the teaching profession with us. They have the expertise and the professional approach. To the teachers I would say that you must satisfy the parents and industry that what you are doing meets their requirements and the needs of our children. For if the public is not convinced then the profession will be laying up trouble for itself in the future'.

James Callaghan, 1976.

Prophetic and powerful words. In fairness to the teaching profession, they too were overtaken by the pace of change from the 1950s and had not necessarily wanted to remain in this position of complete control over what and how the nation's children were taught. Callaghan's Ruskin speech provided ammunition for the developing agenda of the 1980s which had at its core, not only improvements to schools and teaching within the existing framework, but a whole new way of thinking about the responsibility for such decisions. The Department of Education and Science (DES) followed up the Ruskin speech with a Circular to schools instructing local authorities (LAs) to report on the curriculum situation in their own backyards. In a new spirit of openness the results were published in 1979 and were not an encouraging read. Practice varied widely and some authorities had little idea of what went on in their schools.

The case for a core curriculum, as first publicly proposed by Callaghan, to ensure continuity, especially between primary and secondary phases, and breadth and balance was something which many would have signed up to, including teachers. Led by the Government, the Schools' Council and HMI the debate was steered by discussion papers produced by a range of agencies and interests. It is important to remember that in the 1980s HMI remained independent in practice as well as in theory; they constituted a highly respected body of experts. Both the DES and HMI published documents on the curriculum, with HMI's series, *Curriculum Matters*, receiving better reviews due to its less prescriptive and centralist approach. The DES published *The School Curriculum* in 1981. The Schools' Council published their document *The Practical Curriculum* in the same year. Both the DES and the Schools' Council reports called for a greater compulsory component than was currently the case. Pressure was kept up on LAs to work on their curriculum arrangements with two official prompts in 1981. Schools were finally required to publish their curriculum statements (which were determined by headteachers) by the Education Act of 1986.

In 1985, HMI published further deliberations on the curriculum for five to 16 year-olds[8]. It spoke of areas of learning and experience as well as the need for transfer of knowledge and skills and made clear that teaching in discrete subject areas, in secondary schools in particular, militated against a coherent and 'joined up' educational journey for the pupil. Readers who think the proposals later in this book unpalatable might find *Curriculum Matters* an instructive read. It would give a perspective to the statutory materials produced in the intervening decades.

The 1980s debate on the curriculum had a number of themes. One was how to ensure pupils received a broad and balanced education and whether to achieve this compulsion was necessary or whether government encouragement would suffice. Another was whether an argument for compulsion should stretch across the curriculum or be limited to the basic subjects. The Government published a White Paper entitled *Better Schools* in 1985[9], which suggested that broad agreement on the objectives and content of the curriculum would raise standards. It spoke of LAs working with schools to produce a local curriculum model and, endorsing the principles of breadth, balance, relevance and differentiation, tentatively outlined a possible list of purposes for learning. Interestingly, it went on to state that the description of the curriculum content in terms of subject areas was 'a convenience', and furthermore 'it is not in dispute that the purposes of education go beyond learning the traditional subjects'. Unfortunately, the White Paper's thinking on the curriculum was not built on in a way that realised this harmonious model of curriculum development, which could see beyond subject specialisms.

A context for the debate was the growing impatience of the Government with the 'educational establishment' in general, and teachers in particular. One sign of this was the abolition of the Schools' Council in 1984, signalling the end of extensive teacher involvement in curriculum matters at a national and strategic level. Teachers' unions became a serious annoyance to the Government from 1984 due to a protracted national dispute over pay and conditions. Ultimately, the Government decided that it should use its Parliamentary majority to resolve both the union and the curriculum issues.

But government and the teaching profession were not only concerned with curriculum issues. The 1980s saw the growth of a parallel debate on terminal assessment at the compulsory school leaving age. Comprehensive schools, educating pupils of all abilities, required an exam for all abilities. The difficulty of dividing the sheep ('O' Level pupils) from the goats (CSE) was becoming increasingly unpalatable to teachers. Surprisingly, it was probably the most academic Secretary of State for education, Sir Keith Joseph, who listened to, and accepted, the profession's argument for a universal exam and resulted in the amalgamation of 'O' Levels and CSEs in 1986 to form the new GCSE qualification. The GCSE was designed to cover most of the ability range and to provide a coherent set of qualifications and levels of award that were clearly understood by parents, pupils and employers. Although the GCSE was successful in these aspirations, its equivalence at the higher grades with 'O' Level standards has been contested since its inception.

Having moved on assessment, the Government decided to act on the curriculum. The Education Reform Act of 1988 was a landmark piece of education legislation. The most important education Act since 1944 it gave a whole raft of new powers to the Secretary of State, bringing in, amongst other things, national testing and assessment and the local management of schools. Most importantly from our point of view, the Act instituted the new national curriculum. It could be argued that this was a logical conclusion to the debate of the previous decade: if an agreed curriculum would raise standards then why shouldn't schools be required to comply? From there it was all too easy, despite the misgivings of Margaret Thatcher, the Prime Minister of the time, to define 'broad and balanced' subjects with an established panel of 'experts' to fill in the minute detail.

In principle, the idea of a national curriculum attracted very wide, though not quite unanimous support. The argument for an entitlement for all was strongly supported, as was the acceptance that the entitlement ought to have legislative backing. Evidence from HMI and elsewhere that the locally determined curriculum was not meeting need had been broadly accepted. Consensus declined, however, as the process of curriculum design progressed between 1987 and 1989.

The content of the proposed national curriculum owed more to the past than to the future. It was almost entirely concerned with subject content. The ten subjects, eleven in Wales, were decided upon by the Secretary of State, Kenneth Baker, based on principles to which none were privy; however, Denis Lawton, of the University of London Institute of Education, described the selection as 'the reincarnation of the 1904 Secondary Regulations'[10]. Certainly, the subjects bore close resemblance to those on offer by a typical grammar school and reflected ministerial prejudice. There was no room for Social and Political Studies, rapidly expanding in secondary schools at the time. The tendency to relegate craft skills was endorsed. Five other areas, which had been identified as important for all but did not equate to traditional 'subjects': careers education and guidance, health education, education for citizenship, environmental education and economic and industrial awareness, were tacked on as 'cross-curricular themes'.

The aims of the curriculum were curtly summarised in the Act, and appeared as an afterthought rather than the basis for detailed development. Schools were required to provide a broad and balanced curriculum that:

- promoted the spiritual, moral, cultural, mental and physical development of pupils at school and in society;
- prepared pupils for the opportunities, responsibilities and experiences of adult life.

This was a great opportunity lost. Despite all the thinking and writing in the preceding years, and despite the creation (much regretted by 1986) of a largely comprehensive secondary system, the Government did not design a curriculum from first principles. It did not start from a statement of aim. It did not try to anticipate educational needs for the future. It replicated a secondary school structure familiar to members of the Government and its core supporters. The Government simply did not address the question of whether a Century old formula remained appropriate and there was no detailed rationale for a ten-subject curriculum. It could have been sketched out on the back of an envelope.

What followed, however, resulted in a mass of bureaucracy. The Government allowed itself to be convinced that subject content should be defined in detail. The structure of the Programmes of Study and Levels of Attainment, which included 297 statements of attainment in maths and no fewer than 407 in science, was designed by committees consisting of the great and the good from various subject areas, but few teachers. It was huge and unmanageable, especially at primary level. It's not difficult to foresee that appointing a committee of experts to design a syllabus for their pet subject would result in something that might fill the entire waking hours of the poor pupil at the receiving end. There was no single overarching body with the authority to trim the subject groups' ambitions or to regulate their overall size and balance. Indeed, the separate subject groups were instructed not to talk to each other!

From the beginning it was intended that a national curriculum would be subject to national testing and used for accountability and parent (consumer) information. The Task Group on Assessment and Testing (TGAT) arrived at a model, which received general acclaim from the education world but was not entirely to the liking of some of the Conservative Party, including Margaret Thatcher. The TGAT's report was accepted, but its recommendations were grossly distorted by the Schools' Examination and Assessment Council, the Government quango charged with implementing its recommendations. This resulted in a simple, but wholly inadequate model of testing, based on levels of attainment and was tied to key stages across the entire range of national curriculum subjects.

Once the new curriculum was implemented in 1989 it quickly became apparent that a monstrosity had been born. It was simply too large to fit into the time available, particularly at key stages 2 and 4. However, part of the difficulty of implementation was the changed mood of teachers. Having been shocked at the removal of their unions' right to negotiate on pay and conditions in 1987, most were dismayed by the provisions and direction of the Education Reform Act, with its steps towards atomisation and marketisation of the system. As far as the curriculum was concerned, Margaret Thatcher had scored another triumph in her attack on the closed shop of professionalism. Teachers who were prepared to accept the principle of entitlement to a balanced curriculum were horrified at the bureaucracy and workload connected with the hugely detailed prescription and the testing regime. Teachers became sullen. The model wouldn't work, said many educationists. Many teachers were determined to prove them right.

Neither should it be forgotten that the national curriculum was a substantial challenge to the expertise of many primary teachers. Naturally, they had tended to spend more time on subject areas they knew about and less time on areas they didn't. Maths, aspects of science and technology, were all subjects in which many primary teachers lacked confidence. No wonder they were uneasy, especially in the absence of sufficient training opportunities.

Within a year, the National Curriculum Council, the new agency responsible for the curriculum, called a range of expert conferences that gave the clear message that change was necessary. In January 1991, the then Secretary of State, Kenneth Clarke, announced changes. Kenneth Clarke had already illustrated an intrinsic problem of the detailed determination of the curriculum by the state by making an entirely unilateral decision that schools should not include events in modern history that occurred within 20 years. Some of the foundation subjects became optional at key stage 4, and the science and mathematics regulations were to be revised.

But it was not only the size and detailed content of the curriculum that caused the teaching profession difficulties; the proposed assessment arrangements were also heavily criticised. This led in the autumn of 1991 to a substantial revision of the standard assessment test (SAT) at key stages 1 and 3 and of assessment at GCSE. However, teachers were not pacified by this and protests reached a climax in 1993; as the first SATs approached teachers boycotted the tests for seven and 14 year-olds.

John Patten, the then Secretary of State for Education, was forced to set up a review of the national curriculum. He set out four key issues: the scope for slimming down the curriculum, the future of the 10-level scale of attainment, how to simplify the testing arrangements and how to improve the administration of the national curriculum and the tests. The review was led by Sir Ron Dearing, Chair of the School Curriculum and Assessment Authority (SCAA). Its report pointed out that part of the problem of curriculum overload stemmed from the fact that the original working groups were not able to judge their collective weight in terms of teaching the curriculum as a whole. This was compounded by the attempt to spell out the requirements of each national curriculum subject at a level of prescription that many teachers found unacceptably constricting. Dearing recommended slimming down the national curriculum by dividing each subject into essential core and optional material. He claimed that this would release the equivalent of one day per week of curriculum time in key stages 1 to 3 for schools to use at their own discretion. Dearing also recommended that there should be a five-year moratorium on further change after this reform. The Government accepted the report and asked the SCAA to set up advisory groups to see through the changes. Teachers and headteachers comprised at least half their membership, reflecting the importance attached to gaining acceptability amongst the profession, and the new subject regulations, which commenced in September 1995 for key stages 1 to 3, were cut in length from 100,000 to 65,000 words and from 330 to 220 pages. However, although the changes were generally welcomed, this was in the context of what they replaced. The suggestion that the national curriculum would occupy only 80% of the timetable turned out to be a mirage and without a doubt, the most popular element of the review was the moratorium. This, too, was a kind of mirage as the General Election of 1997 returned a new government with their own set of ideas.

When the Labour Party regained power most teachers had little idea what to expect but they were probably not expecting the previous party's policies written large. New Labour emphasised the need for park keepers in the secret garden: teachers and schools needed to be more accountable to parents, pupils, LAs and to the Government. In the past, too much poor quality teaching had gone unchecked. With the reform of public services a major element of the Prime Minister's narrative, it was inevitable that teachers' desire to be left alone was to be frustrated, although the Government was careful not to break the letter of the moratorium.

The Labour Government used more vigorously still the tools it had inherited for centralised control of teachers and teaching. Continuing acceptance of the right of government to determine curriculum content and assessment led to a drift towards government control over pedagogy; the final teachers' bastion to come under attack. David Blunkett, the comparatively long-serving Secretary of State, imposed his own clear views from the start. They included the necessity for greater emphasis on 'the basics', in this case literacy and numeracy, the addition of a new subject: citizenship, and the need for an unprecedented training programme imposing a standard pedagogy.

Blunkett told primary schools to cut the time spent on history, geography, design and technology, art, music and PE in order to spend one hour per day each on literacy and numeracy. Teachers were told to 'have regard to' the programmes of study but were no longer required to comply with them. At the same time the Government, either naively or cynically, told primary schools to 'maintain a broad and balanced curriculum'. The Government used a carrot and stick approach to ensure its will was implemented. Building on Conservative initiatives the Primary Literacy Strategy (1998) and the Primary Numeracy Strategy (1999) became the largest and most intensive professional development programmes ever run in a major education system. If they were the carrot, the stick was the threat that OfSTED would judge any school not using the standard literacy and numeracy hours.

This was a faintly sinister method of controlling a public service. Ostensibly the literacy and numeracy hours were not compulsory but by the late nineties OfSTED had built up such a negative reputation in the minds of teachers and headteachers that to declare any policy the focus of inspection was in practice the equivalent of statute. To this day, OfSTED is at the hub of a machine whose business is to churn out orthodoxy and compliance, whilst pretending that it is an independent body interested only in quality, washing its hands of its own effects on school practice.

It must be said that whilst the literacy and numeracy strategies were received negatively in principle as an attack on professionalism, in practice they were more positively received, especially in the case of numeracy as teachers felt the strategy methods improved their teaching. Retrospectively, the strategies are seen as having improved the skill level in primary school classrooms, although the academic evaluation was ambivalent about the longer-term benefits. It was also clear this programme could not be a sustainable model for pedagogical development.

Blunkett then moved on to another review of the national curriculum with the aim to move towards a more flexible, less prescriptive framework within which key priorities, such as literacy and numeracy, were fully recognised whilst taking account of the role of the curriculum in preparing people for the opportunities, responsibilities and experiences of adult life. He evaded the moratorium commitment with a timetable in which changes would not be implemented until 2000, and by implying that change would be minimal.

For Curriculum 2000, the two aims which informed the curriculum from its inception were developed by means of revised wording and a substantial gloss:

- the school curriculum should aim to provide opportunities for all pupils to learn and achieve;
- the school curriculum should aim to promote pupils' spiritual, moral, social and cultural development and prepare all pupils for the opportunities, responsibilities and experiences of life.

A careful reading of them still failed to make it clear how they cohered with a curriculum based on nineteenth century subject divisions, although they were in line with the introduction of Blunkett's pet subject, citizenship. Introduced as a result of widespread fear that young people were growing up devoid of social and personal responsibility it became an add-on, with few teachers or schools understanding how it should be implemented. In part, this was an attempt to replace the failed cross-curricular themes of the original national curriculum. The process had become similar to making poorly thought through modifications to a house that no longer meets the owner's needs: it's comfortable and familiar in parts, but difficult to find one's way round and from the outside it looks a mess.

Also in 2000, non-statutory guidance was issued on the teaching of personal, health, and social education. There seemed to be obvious duplication between social education and citizenship, but in the years since this has mattered little, since both subjects have been largely marginalised in most schools. There is no incentive for primary schools to take them seriously; they do not contribute to key stage 2 performance tables. There is no incentive for secondary schools to take them seriously; the half a GCSE available for citizenship is of little help with the performance tables. The same could be said for the new Equalities Statement. Excellent in itself, few teachers are aware of its existence and its impact on practice has been unnoticeable.

There were other changes at either end of the schools' age range. GCE 'A' Level was reformed, with a haste that led to serious difficulties, into a two-stage qualification. And the foundation stage was introduced for children from age three to the end of the reception year, with a framework of six areas of learning rather than subjects: personal, social and emotional development, communication, language and literacy, mathematical development, knowledge and understanding of the world, physical and creative development.

It might be assumed that this process of continual reform of the statutory curriculum would result in better learning experiences in classrooms. It might be expected that reform would retain the important principles that had achieved consensus in the eighties, whilst ditching the details that were unpopular and further adjusting the content to meet professional concerns about the gap between the curriculum and the needs of pupils. These assumptions are incorrect.

The Dearing review solved a political problem by reducing the size of the curriculum, but misunderstood the principles of assessment and retained a highly prescribed model which left teachers with little leeway. Curriculum 2000 attempted to add some *post-facto* coherence to a model that fatally lacked coherence due to its subject-based construction. Throughout the life of the national curriculum, ministers have insisted on inserting their own pet interests. Yet its intrinsic problems have left teachers frustrated at the lack of engagement of pupils.

This becomes more obvious as we pass through the key stages. The Government has been forced to respond to the demands from secondary schools to be freed from the demands of key stage 4, but true to the history of the national curriculum this has been done in piecemeal and contradictory ways. Typical is the mess over teaching of modern foreign languages. Faced with evidence that this was unpopular with pupils at key stage 4, the Government abolished the compulsion. Soon, and completely unsurprisingly, the number of GCSE candidates reduced sharply. Then the Government decided this was a bad thing and called on, well who but Dearing, to try to clear up the mess it had created.

What secondary schools really wanted was a much more complete review of the curriculum. For many, the shortage of what is usually called vocational options made it impossible to meet pupils' needs. A chance arose in 2004 to make a radical change which would perhaps have brought at least part of the curriculum into alignment with its stated aims: an independent review led by Sir Mike Tomlinson with DfES support. A diploma programme for all was envisaged which broke down barriers between vocational and academic learning, redesigned and reduced assessment and gave greater scope for individualised learning. Tomlinson, like Dearing an experienced fixer, took care to build consensual support for his proposals, but at the final moment the employers' organisations, followed by the Conservative Party, broke ranks. It proved too radical a vision, and has been downsized in scope and potential impact into a new system of vocational diplomas.

It is clear that many educationists continue to hope that another opportunity will arise to put into place a system at least similar to the Tomlinson proposals. For some, the Specialised Diploma could be developed in this way, although this is clearly not the current intention of the Government, which remains committed to the retention of GCSE and 'A' Level with the Diploma as an alternative.

However, dissatisfaction with the current arrangements remains, and debate is growing. Recently, the QCA, which has the twin and potentially conflicting roles of supporting and defending the curriculum and assessment arrangements it put into place whilst arguing for necessary change, has much more clearly signalled that the current curriculum model is inappropriate. It has revised the national curriculum programmes of study for key stage 3, to take effect in 2008. The revised programmes of study have been designed to provide greater flexibility for teachers, a greater coherence for the curriculum as a whole and increased personalisation of the curriculum for learners, taking into account the newer priorities such as the *Every Child Matters* agenda and personal, learning and thinking skills.

These revised programmes of study have a uniform format with a less specific content and encourage teachers to help their pupils develop a deeper understanding of the key concepts and processes underpinning the subject. They outline key processes, the range and content of the subject from which the areas of study should be drawn, and the curriculum opportunities that pupils should be given. Nevertheless, ministers have again been unable to resist intervening, making demands about the detail of content of both English and history.

The QCA intends that having a common format to the programmes will allow schools to make connections between the subjects and make the curriculum more coherent for pupils by, for example, including references to critical understanding in almost all subjects to enable pupils to develop critical understanding of communications, of the environment and of themselves.

Other key ideas include providing opportunities for developing pupils' creativity and adaptability and enabling them to see how their studies relate to the world beyond the classroom by their learning outside in museums and sports centres and through contact with, for example, artists and writers.

The reform of key stage 3 is clearly the most radical development since the introduction of the national curriculum. Its effect should be to reduce detailed prescription, increase coherence, concentrate on principles, and allow teachers to make their own judgements on content to a much greater extent than present. In the following chapters, we develop our criticism of the present system and suggest an alternative. There is no doubt that the new key stage 3 will be a step in the direction we propose, but how great that step will be remains to be seen.

So what can we learn from this brief history? Apart from the rather ineffective Schools' Council, teachers collectively have never had a proper opportunity to make the curriculum other than at school level. Where they have done so, Mode 3 CSE and the TVEI initiative in the 1980s, it has often been of good quality and has led to more inclusive and relevant experience for their pupils. Prior to 1988, the problem was that good practice was seldom widely disseminated and poor practice was seldom checked.

Within a few years, teachers in England have moved from a very high degree of autonomy to a very high degree of prescription; they have moved from matters of what to teach and how to assess pupils to matters of how to teach. Teachers have therefore moved from the secret garden to minute control and scrutiny.

The idea that individual teachers ought to have complete independence to decide what to teach has been discredited in an age of accountability. The idea that such decisions are of sufficient importance to merit statutory provision became consensual, and remains so. But this consensus in favour of a national curriculum has not been translated into support for *the* national curriculum, which as originally constructed went from one extreme to the other. As we reach the twentieth anniversary of its birth, there is a clear need for a debate. True, the very fact of an all-embracing and all-detailed curriculum has deterred teachers from this debate, but now questions of control and accountability need fresh thinking. Should the professionals have more say in what is taught? How can a statutory curriculum reflect the interests of all stakeholders, local and national? What about pupil voice? Can we avoid an intrinsic danger that arises from the fact that a national curriculum is a state curriculum, and a state curriculum is a political curriculum? So far, ministerial interference, sometimes at the level of detail, has been a feature.

What we propose in the following chapters tries to take account both of the value of local innovation and the proper requirement for accountability. We also try to contribute to the debate that has begun and will no longer be limited by official pronouncements on the official curriculum; a debate which should have been the starting point for the national curriculum but wasn't, a debate from first principles about what school leavers need and should know in the twenty-first century.

References

1 Central Advisory Council for Education. 1959. *The Crowther Report: Fifteen to Eighteen*. Her Majesty's Stationary Office, London.

2 Bassey, M. 2005. *Teachers and government: a history of intervention in education*. ATL, London.

3 Kelly, A.V. 1987. Education: The made simple series. Heinemann, Oxford.

4 Central Advisory Council for Education. 1963. *Half our future*. Her Majesty's Stationary Office, London.

5 Central Advisory Council for Education. 1967. *Children and their primary schools*. Her Majesty's Stationary Office, London.

6 Her Majesty's Inspectorate. 1978. *Primary education in England: A survey by HMI*. Her Majesty's Stationary Office, London.

7 Dunford, J. 1998. *Her Majesty's Inspectorate of Schools Since 1944*. Woburn Press, London.

8 Her Majesty's Inspectorate. 1985. *The Curriculum from 5–16. Curriculum Matters 2*. Her Majesty's Stationary Office, London.

9 The Department of Education and Science. 1985. *Better Schools*. Her Majesty's Stationary Office, London.

10 Gillard, D. 2004. *Education in England: a brief history* taken from http://www.dg.dial.pipex.com/history/text.shtml.

CHAPTER FOUR

A new national curriculum

We have concluded that the arguments for a national curriculum remain compelling, but the present model does not fit the bill. In the next two chapters we take a blank piece of paper and sketch out a model that does fit the bill. The first step must be to decide the coverage and detail of the new national curriculum. Should it specify the whole content covered by schools? Should the content be specified in detail or should it just give headings as in the Swedish model? The arguments for a national curriculum advanced earlier do not lead to any particular conclusion regarding its coverage. This is as much a political decision as the content and it makes sense that totalitarian governments would wish to specify the entire school curriculum and provide detailed elaboration. One would expect western 'liberal' governments to be less prescriptive.

In the case of England, although there can be endless arguments about the selection of subjects, there is no doubt that the original structure met the conventional demand for a broad and balanced curriculum. The problem of coverage arose because of the inability of the subject committees to keep within their briefs in respect of the time allocation for their subject at each key stage, despite them claiming they had. As we have seen, the Government was relieved when its supreme fixer, Dearing, produced a solution which was accepted by the profession and its unions, although there was no attempt to explain why 80% was an appropriate time allocation for the national curriculum.

There is a natural tendency in modern open societies for a national curriculum to be under pressure from the whole range of interest groups, each of which believes that its subject is so important that every child ought to learn about it. In assuming the power to determine a curriculum, a government is taking responsibility to arbitrate between these groups.

If they use a knowledge model there is another, even more fundamental problem for curriculum designers. Knowledge is expanding at an astonishing, if not frightening, rate. Some of it is just extra detail of a known framework, but much of it is not. This gives rise to two separate problems. One is the increased difficulty of selection from an escalating number of items. Secondly, the need for a dynamic model of curriculum development whereas change to a national curriculum is always laborious and bureaucratic. Whilst it is right to treat government decisions on the learning of every child in this country with due deliberation and wide consultation it makes the national curriculum slow to respond to change. And change is what we have plenty of.

Another cause of overload in a national curriculum is that ministers sometimes add their own enthusiasms to the pot. It must be very tempting for a politician with power and strong views to argue that their electoral mandate authorises such intervention. We saw in the previous chapter how ministers have succumbed to temptation; some of their changes welcomed others less so. From the perspective of the present discussion, the problem with additions is the lack of subtractions to balance them.

It may sometimes be difficult to resist the claims for an item to be added to the national curriculum. But how much more difficult is it to decide to remove an item? Previous painstaking procedures led to a ministerial decision that an item was so important that the law should declare that it should be taught to every child, how likely then is it that this item will ever be removed? No wonder we have had very little subtraction since Dearing.

So in England most of the pressure has been to add items to the curriculum rather than remove them. As we saw, when the Government decided to impose greater emphasis on English and maths on primary schools, it avoided the overcrowding argument by removing the requirement to comply in full with the programmes of study for the foundation subjects. The result in primary schools has been to narrow the curriculum, which calls into question the important principle of an entitlement to a broad and balanced experience. It is difficult to see how the overcrowding tendency can be avoided if the curriculum is defined in detail.

Most schools in England claim that they have no time left over after meeting the demands of the national curriculum. Many teachers claim that overcrowding is such as to damage pedagogy, by requiring coverage of the programme of study at such a pace that there is no time to go down interesting by-ways when they open up during lessons. If these perceptions are unjustified the Government and its agencies need to consider what has caused them and how to alter them. Another possibility is that the 'overcrowding' is really no more than a welcome injection of pace into teaching and learning. But if perceptions of overcrowding are justified, does it matter?

There are some good reasons why a national curriculum should not dictate the entire content. The first is the queasy feeling of association with the totalitarian state. The second is that since change is somewhat ponderous, it would be unfortunate if there were no space for a faster curriculum response to events. The third is that a 100% national curriculum precludes schools from responding to local circumstances. For example, Russia is overcoming this problem in its current reforms by specifying approximately 75% of the curriculum nationally, 10% regionally and 10% by the school. The fourth is altogether more substantial. English schools have a tradition of school level curriculum innovation. Curriculum innovation by teachers at local level is important for a number of reasons. It requires teachers to reflect deeply on their pupils' learning needs and their own teaching, thus using higher order skills and knowledge other than the craft skills required to 'deliver' a lesson. It produces and reproduces a vital stock of expertise in curriculum design, without which it is difficult to see where the next generation of national curriculum designers will come from. Potentially it provides a point of contact between the school and the community if the innovation is in response to a local need or draws on local resources. And it creates a sense of dynamism in schools. A 100% national curriculum, however, creates a sense of stasis.

Newly qualified teachers in England are now often described, as much by their schools as by the trainers, as the best ever. As technicians, they know the specified curriculum and can deliver quality lessons in standard formats. Yet the present generation of teachers have not learnt to question what young people need to know or be able to do, and they do not expect to play a part in providing answers. The collective capacity of the profession to speculate about such things and to try out new answers continues to diminish. It is therefore becoming increasingly urgent to create the space in which this trend can be reversed, that space must be a less than 100% national curriculum.

The tendency towards overcrowding seems unavoidable in a system in which there is both detailed content specification and active competition for inclusion of new items. So is there a way to create the necessary space?

The answer may lie in reducing the detail of the specification, and there may be two ways of doing this. Both involve dealing with the issue of 'the subject', as discussed earlier.

The Early Years Foundation Stage is described in terms of six areas of learning and development rather than subjects. In the 2007 version they comprise personal, social and emotional development; communication, language and literacy; problem solving, reasoning and numeracy; knowledge and understanding of the world; physical development; and creative development.

A curriculum defined in terms of 'ways of knowing', or 'areas of learning and experience' or 'areas of learning and development' is one in which the emphasis moves from the detailed knowledge content of subjects to their principles, concepts and skills. The national curriculum already contains elements of this approach. School history, for example, concentrates strongly on gathering evidence, comparing sources and an understanding of the social construction of history. Design technology emphasises the processes of design, some say so much that the skills of 'making' are being sidelined. However, in such areas the national curriculum specifies not only these principles but also the knowledge through which they are to be manifested.

It would be possible to design a national curriculum at a higher level of generality, solely in terms of principles concepts and attitudes. Such a specification, being general, would not in itself determine the taught time required. There is, however, a substantial drawback to a curriculum specified at this level of generality: it creates severe difficulty in designing any national assessment. A standardised test of an area of learning, whether it aims to reward primarily understanding of the principles or knowledge of some detail, must inevitably be based on some knowledge. That knowledge must be specified in the programme of study.

There is an alternative approach. The approach suggested here is to move away from defining the curriculum in terms of knowledge, whether generally defined as ways of knowing or as detailed knowledge content, and to replace it with a definition in terms of skills. The idea of a skills-based curriculum is discussed next.

Advocates of a skills-based curriculum stress the 'can do' in the description of a curriculum as what learners 'know, understand and can do'. This is the approach followed in this book, but it is not without its doubters, and is certainly open to misunderstanding. What follows is an account of what a skills curriculum is and what it isn't.

First, it is clear that there is an inextricable link between knowing, understanding and doing. The boundary between 'knowing how to' (as understanding) and 'being able to do' (as a skill) is fuzzy, perhaps even artificial. However, although this close relationship may give rise to difficulty at the boundary, in everyday use the distinction is both possible and useful. Take riding a bike. To actually ride a bike you have to know 'how' to do it, which requires learning, but the average cyclist does not require high-level mental input prior to each cycle ride. But can it be said that the cyclist is practising a skill? And by the way, there is a good argument for including cycling in a skills curriculum. The question is rather whether it is important enough to be included in a national curriculum.

Two frequent misunderstandings about a skills curriculum need clarification at the start. Both assume partial coverage of the total skills needed by tomorrow's society.

The first derives from an assumption that the outcome of a skills-based design will be not very different from present good practice in classrooms. It does not question the overall emphasis on the academic, or intellectual. Education is assumed to be primarily about the development of the mind. On this misunderstanding, curriculum designers start from the usual list of academic disciplines, and seek to analyse the skills that form their various methodologies. This brings us back to the earlier discussion of forms of knowledge defined as 'ways of knowing', which involves not just facts, or even just understanding, but also knowing how to discover, analyse, codify and verify knowledge within a specified area. Surely this is a good example of the close but conceptually separable relationship between knowledge and skills, because these are often described as 'subject skills'. Some critics of the skills approach place 'subject skills' in the 'knowledge' box and assume they would not be covered. We are putting them in the skills box and assuming they will be.

The second misunderstanding relates to an even more limited perspective. Some assume that a skills curriculum is an employment-facing curriculum. There are good reasons to make this assumption. In the vocational education and training arena, course specification and assessment are usually designed in terms of skills, or often as competencies. Further, most current discussion of curriculum reform in popular and political circles is a highly intellectually confused assertion of the need for 'vocational education' at secondary level. It is hardly surprising that when politicians normally justify spending on education, by way of references to international economic competitiveness, there is a common assumption that a skills curriculum is a skills-needed-by-employers curriculum. It is not easy to discover exactly what the skills needed by employers are, from the statements of employers' organisations certainly, but there appears to be some consensus around lists of so-called 'soft skills' and 'desired attributes' such as communication skills, personal and interpersonal skills (teamwork, initiative and flexibility) and so on.

However, there are close similarities between personal skills and the outcomes sought in curriculum areas such as personal and social education and citizenship. These soft skills or competencies have been considered traditionally to be a by-product of schools' routines and relationships. It seems that the generic skills needed by people in their economic roles turn out to be very similar to those needed in their roles as citizens, in their families and in their leisure time.

In this book, a skills curriculum is not meant to be limited to academic subject skills, although it includes them. Neither is it limited to work-related skills, although it includes them too. What is proposed here is to produce an analysis of what school leavers in the twenty-first century need. A new national curriculum should place under one umbrella the whole range of outcomes for all pupils expected by the state. The major difference from previous curriculum models is that it should consider the needs of the whole person without assuming that the academic or intellectual aspects should have a higher status than the others. The first truly comprehensive curriculum should rebalance the academic, situated in the mind, against those parts of humanity situated in the body, the heart and the soul. Curricula may well be designed by people for whom the mind predominates, but those designers should see that the twenty-first century requires a population with higher levels of social, emotional and moral performance, and a regenerated capacity for doing and making.

Christ Church School, Bexley

Along with seven other schools, Christ Church School designed a new curriculum entitled *The Creative Learning Journey*. This curriculum is a skills continuum and took the foundation stage six areas of learning from nursery through to year six. Pupils were motivated by the use of such a skills-based continuum and topics were adaptable. Pupils were not assessed using rigorous tests, but by observing how pupils utilise their skills independently.

The headteacher helped the school to embrace *The Creative Learning Journey* curriculum, which meant that they no longer used QCA units. Teachers and pupils alike were enthusiastic about the new curriculum and embraced the new way of learning.

We need a bit of honesty in this analysis. Most people are not intellectuals. Most people do not live their lives predominantly in the abstract. It is not clear that it would be preferable to do otherwise; the world cannot survive only through thought. It is more appropriate now to move towards encouraging action based on understanding. Yet throughout the world, education systems are based on the considered superiority of the abstract over the real, of thought over action. This is because mass education systems developed in the twentieth century copied the curriculum considered necessary for social elites; leisured classes who could afford and valued such attitudes.

Britain is not alone in failing to think through what would be useful learning when presented with eleven years of compulsory education. Most attempts to deal with this issue have led to the differentiation of the curriculum, often with segregated provision. The widely drawn conclusion that we need to return to differentiation is a major error that our proposals try to address.

This plea for a curriculum based on a wide range of skills is bound to be misinterpreted, if not misrepresented, so it may be worth our getting in some denials. This way of thinking is not anti-intellectual. The skills of metacognition, of interpreting, codifying and evaluating knowledge are becoming increasingly important and we cannot leave it to chance that young people learn how to think metacognitively. To repeat, this kind of curriculum would not be anti-knowledge; it would simply promote knowledge transformation over knowledge transmission. A comprehensive curriculum would reduce the proportion of time spent on knowledge transmission; there would be time for skills connected with all aspects of humanity including the intellectual. What this might look like may become clearer when those skills are discussed in more detail later.

Mayplace School, Bexley

Mayplace School is another school affiliated with *The Creative Learning Journey*. Here the headteacher began the journey by organising a series of 'focus weeks' that took place at the end of each half term. During these weeks staff planned the teaching and learning around a theme and skills-based activities were used to address all areas of the curriculum. The introduction of the new curriculum has empowered staff and motivated pupils. Pupils are interested in discovering things for themselves. The introduction of *The Creative Learning Journey* was so successful that Mayplace School implemented the new curriculum from nursery to year six in September 2006.

To supporters of a comprehensive curriculum, there are plenty of trends in current education debate and practice which appear to point towards this change. Here we discuss two. The first is the Labour Government's *Every Child Matters* (ECM) policies. It must be said that ECM sits uneasily with other areas of policy; indeed, for some time this was literally true, in the sense that the policy was jointly owned by two government departments before being placed less ambiguously within the DfES.

Schools have been placed under the duty to promote the five outcomes of ECM:

- be healthy;
- stay safe;
- enjoy and achieve;
- make a positive contribution;
- achieve economic well-being.

No one would suggest that this comprises a model for a comprehensive curriculum, but it widens the required angle of vision of schools, after a period of unrelenting single-minded attention to 'standards'. It endorses a perspective of a pupil as a person. This may appear unexceptional, but coming after an orthodoxy where pupils are treated as test-takers it represents a welcome change in some schools, or it would do if the standards pressure were to be lifted.

Part of the strategy for ensuring the achievement of the five outcomes for all is the provision of extended services. This highlights a major distinction between ECM and educational aims. Although extended services are to be largely based on school sites, it is not useful to see them as provided by schools. Better, they may be seen as services aimed at removing barriers to learning, and thus in support of schools. This formulation makes clear that any desired learning outcomes for pupils need to be specified in the curriculum and taught during the normal school day. It also provides a presumption that there are elements of the five outcomes which link to desired learning outcomes. The significance of this for the present discussion is that they are not academic outcomes but concerned with wider aspects of the learner as a developing member of society. In short, ECM provides a reminder that the curriculum needs to contain a wide range of learning needs for people in the twenty-first century.

The second policy area which should provide pointers for new thinking on the curriculum is the 14-19 agenda. The Government's own version of 14-19 reform starts from the analysis of problems of performance and participation at age 16 and beyond as described earlier. The positive aspect of this policy is that it accepts that the secondary curriculum offer is inadequate. Its weakness is that it restricts this admission to a proportion of pupils at key stage 4. The problem with the analysis is that it only partially describes the disengagement of secondary aged pupils, and as a result prescribes a solution which is far too limited. It falls into the trap described above of equating a skills-based curriculum with a 'vocational curriculum'.

A comprehensive curriculum would contain few, if any, areas of understanding and skill that do not already get a mention in the current national curriculum. The difference is in the balance and the assessment, which we come to later. After all, one purpose of a national curriculum is to provide breadth and balance, and as we have seen balance has been entirely absent.

A comprehensive curriculum recognises humanity as physical beings. It would, for example, recognise that even though we don't live on a diet of just bread, we should all know how to plant, grow and harvest wheat, how to distribute it, market it and make palatable meals from it. Everyone, not just the farm labourer's child, needs to know how to grow plants in a changing climate as well as to learn horticulture, how to cook and food values. Science is not to be abolished, but refocused to provide the knowledge base for practical activity.

A comprehensive curriculum recognises humanity as social beings. It accepts that the world is vulnerable partly because humanity's social and political development has failed to keep pace with technological and economic development. It recognises that everyone needs improved social skills, whether face-to-face or across the globe, and the capacity for tolerance and mutual understanding in a world of potential surplus but actual want. In Britain it also recognises that we all need to develop skills of engagement with the community and commitment to the collective, at local, national and global levels.

A comprehensive curriculum also recognises humanity as individuals and as intellectual beings. It would provide opportunities for all to develop self-understanding and self-expression through the expressive and creative arts, through aspects of philosophy, through thinking and learning and through the skills and methods of academic subjects.

Quethiock Church of England VA School, Cornwall

Pupils at the Quethiock Church of England School have used their creative arts skills to inspire an exciting curriculum and in 2005 pupils displayed their artwork at the local horticultural school. The headteacher recognised that the curriculum for high achieving children lacked coherence, and subjects and units no longer linked together. Initially, pupils were encouraged to become 'experts' on two local artists and then tasked with producing their own artwork, linking literacy and numeracy. The school successfully enriched the curriculum through creative arts, and made learning exciting and engaging whilst celebrating local history and the environment. This and other projects embarked upon by the school have raised pupils' self-esteem and creativity.

And lastly, a comprehensive curriculum recognises that to access fully these skills and understandings we all need some basic skills, especially numeracy, oracy and literacy, but would acquire them integrally with the practice of other skills. The legendary darts player who becomes numerically competent would be a model for the acquisition of these skills.

We call this a comprehensive curriculum because everyone should be entitled to it. There is plenty in it to occupy all pupils throughout their compulsory education. The retreat from the present national curriculum at key stage 4 arose from consumer resistance, particularly from older pupils, rather than any principled critique of the original. This does not provide evidence in favour of differentiation at key stage 4 or at any other. The argument for a differentiated curriculum is that there are different pupils who need different skills and knowledge. The proposition here is that these differences, which are usually considered in terms of preparation for employment, should not arise at compulsory school age.

There is widespread disengagement from the current curriculum and testing system, probably starting in year 5. We are suggesting here that a really broad and truly balanced curriculum would engage the vast majority of young people. This is not only because the curriculum content would be more useful, but also because most of this curriculum demands a pedagogy involving active learners, whether it be doing and making, practising social interaction, or being creative. It demands an end to the passive pupil, a lesson of copying from the board.

The proponents of what they call academic and vocational or general and applied pathways, but are really streams, have to justify the lack of balance in these paths. Is it right that 'academic' pupils should be deprived of full opportunities to develop their physical skills and their understanding of themselves as social beings? Is right that 'vocational' 14 year-olds should be regarded, and thus encouraged to regard themselves, as nothing but young workers?

It has been pointed out already that a curriculum that develops social skills is also a vocational curriculum in that it will develop skills usually identified by employers as important. That generic level is appropriate for pupils of compulsory school age. We agree with the Government, and just about everyone else, that it is important to increase the rate of participation in post-compulsory education and training, in which Britain rates 24 out of 29 OECD countries. Post-16 is the appropriate time for more differentiated learning, with an increased focus on employment.

Of course, a pupil may learn to use woodworking tools and become inspired to be a cabinet-maker. Another may learn the principles of law and determine to become a solicitor. Yet another may learn the plight of disadvantaged families and be inspired to become a community worker. In a broad and balanced skills-based curriculum all pupils would experience all these things, and some would wish to take some of them further as studies, hobbies or careers. But the skills are to be taught to all pupils because all pupils need them, and at compulsory school age the vocational motive should be of secondary importance.

What skills do we have in mind?

Many curriculum thinkers have been here before. There are any number of skills models. Here are some.

The Canadian Prime Minister's Advisory Council on Science and Technology accepted a report from an Expert Panel on Skills on skills and opportunities in the knowledge economy. The panel proposed the following as essential skills:

- basic skills – read, write, calculate and operate basic computer applications;
- effective communication – verbal, written and presentation skills for the purposes of negotiation, persuasion, facilitation, coaching and mentoring;
- thinking skills – think, analyse and solve problems; assess situations, evaluate and implement suggestions;

- team work – co-operate with others and work in teams;
- information literacy – locate, gather analyse and organise information;
- learning habits – adapt to a range of situations; take risks; learn independently, exercise responsibility, innovate.

The International Labour Organisation (2002) defined the role of primary and secondary ('basic') education as 'to ensure to each individual the full deployment of the human personality and citizenship; and to lay the foundation for employability'. It listed the following skills to be provided by basic education institutions:

- minimum requirements – literacy and numeracy;
- foundation skills – the ability to identify, analyse and solve problems; the capacity to learn new skills; computer literacy; simple scientific knowledge and technology;
- social skills – including an understanding of citizenship and the culture of work; an understanding of social rights and claims, and social obligations and responsibilities.

The OECD (2002) maintained a distinction between 'workplace competencies' (tacit knowledge) and basic education (codified knowledge), while recognising their complementary relationship. It offered the following as a list of workplace competencies:

- interpersonal skills – teamwork and the ability to collaborate; leadership capabilities;
- intrapersonal skills – motivation and attitude; the ability to learn; problem-solving skills; effective communication; analytical skills;
- ICT skills.

The qualities and skills that need to be developed in young people to prepare them for life in the information age seem to fall into three categories. First is the area of cognition. This comprises the basic skills of literacy, numeracy, ICT and problem solving, in particular the acquisition and rehearsal of the skills of comprehension, deduction, application and evaluation. Next is the area of intrapersonal or metacognition, which describes the process of analysing one's own learning with a view to making it more efficient. Third are interpersonal skills; the ability to work with others.

While these formulations take us forward, they do not offer the balance we call for. The list below distils elements of recent and not so recent taxonomies. It is not intended as the definitive answer. We do not want to die in the ditch in defence of every last detail. We do not want to retreat from the idea that the reformed curriculum should be defined as a broad and balanced range of skills, but the point of this book is to stimulate more debate. We recognise there is no definitive answer to the question of the contents of a school curriculum.

Let's start with the bit some other models leave out, because it marks out a key difference between traditional curriculum statements and what is needed for a comprehensive curriculum. Much greater prominence needs to be given to what might be described as physical skills of co-ordination, control, manipulation and movement. To be plain: schools must be enabled to place a higher value on *all* pupils progressively developing these skills.

Humanity is marked out from other species, certainly, in the size of its brain, but also by its possession of an opposable thumb. The human hand is able to manipulate the physical world to a degree that can be described as a key characteristic of humanity. To be human means to be able to 'make'.

This may sound far too anthropological for curriculum design in the twenty-first century western world, but we need to consider the essentials of humanity in view of the very rapid pace of economic, social and cultural change. Doing and making have been essential in the struggle for survival for most of human history, but they are also a source of deep human satisfaction. In a society in which, for many, existence is not given a meaning by religion, the achievement of making has more importance in providing meaning.

Making also creates a relationship between the maker and the physical world. For those who are concerned about the future of the planet, in the physical and ecological senses, education must include the establishment of such a relationship. To manipulate materials is to make progress towards understanding the fragility of their availability on present trends.

One way of describing this skill as an element in a national curriculum would be, 'competency in using and working with the physical and material world would enable students to':

- practice and enjoy creative and problem solving activity through making, doing and acting;
- learn how to express themselves intellectually and physically through interacting, playing and working with others.

From an early age, children begin to master physical skills. Initially this is about the ability to control their motor skills, to sit, crawl and walk, to grasp and to let go. Children develop these skills at different rates but we do know that gross motor skills, the large movements that children make when they run and climb, need to be well developed before smaller movements, such as manipulation of fine implements, pencils, scissors will be successful. We also know that, until children have mastered gross motor control, they will find it very difficult to sit still for long periods of time. In the early phases of this curriculum, development of physical control over both gross and fine movements will be important; this development continues throughout life as our range of movement develops, for instance in dance, different forms of sport and crafts.

Not only does the early development of gross motor skills precede fine manual skills but it requires continuous emphasis throughout compulsory schooling; this is another aspect of a rebalanced comprehensive curriculum. The arguments for physical education (PE), intertwined with health education, are commonplace. PE should be given more time and be interpreted much more widely. Physical skills such as walking, which involves a disposition as well as a technique, and digging, should be practised as they are close to the essence of humanity.

Historically, for most people learning how to do and make has been embedded in informal cultural transmission. As economies advanced, learning became partly formalised in guilds and, later, apprenticeships. However, these developments were disconnected from 'education'. Education was an experience limited to the 'educated classes', whose comparative wealth and power freed them from the need to do and make, whose wealth enabled them to enjoy the fruits of others, and whose leisure allowed them to value 'higher' intellectual pursuits. This is the origin of the ideological distinction between mental and manual labour and the consequential distinction between 'academic' and 'vocational', which is therefore deeply imbedded in our culture.

A comprehensive curriculum rebalances the human importance of doing and making against intellectual activity. Earlier, this distinction, between manual and mental, was described as ideological. This is because it only takes a minute's consideration to see that they are interdependent. It is impossible to make something without first thinking about it, unless the operation has been practised so often that it has become automatic, in which case the thought has become an inbuilt resource, often called 'experience'. Indeed, as pointed out elsewhere, this relation is embedded in the 'design and make' concept within national curriculum technology. Yet even here, in practice the mental takes precedence over the manual, the design over the creation. A comprehensive skill-based curriculum must give far more emphasis to the doing and making and must stress the development and practice of fine manual skills.

Sometimes critics of our approach assume that we are advocating a knowledge-free curriculum. This is clearly an impossibility. Somebody wants to saw a piece of wood. They need to know how to make a clean and accurate cut (the skill), but assuming they are not a mindless saw fiend this in itself wouldn't be much use unless they also knew the mathematics of length to enable them to make the cut in the right place, and perhaps something about the qualities of various timbers to use the right kind of wood.

It could be argued that the proposal to emphasise what we call physical skills is not really about the curriculum at all, but about pedagogy. On this argument, there would be nothing wrong with the present curriculum if it were taught through more active learning methods, with pupils spending more time doing and making in order to understand the intellectual content.

Certainly, we seek a more active pedagogy in our schools. We propose to specify physical skills as a major component of a national curriculum because we see them as an end, rather than only a means, and because the point of a written curriculum is to state the learning outcomes most desired. If society decides that skills of doing and making should be learnt by all pupils, than the national curriculum must say so, rather than hoping that they are reflected in methods of teaching and learning.

Children learn to communicate from a very early age. Even very young babies make eye contact and become more alert when a familiar carer speaks to them. Communication skills for young children are about much more than speaking and listening: they are about constructing meaning, understanding body-language, and learning rules of effective conversation. These skills are learnt more quickly in an environment where children know that carers and educators want to hear what they have to say.

South Farnborough Infant School, Hampshire

By the use of curriculum teams, South Farnborough Infant School introduced a new sense of creativity. The headteacher organised staff into three curriculum teams, each with a specific focus. The teams were made up of teachers from each year group, teaching assistants and governors. Team members moved around each other's classes so that they could sample work and offer feedback. Cover and continuity are now no longer a problem and teachers understand the different demands of foundation, year 1 and year 2. The transition from reception to year 1 was identified by staff as significant for children and looked at the six areas of learning. Changes were made to the curriculum to make this transition smoother and the children were encouraged to make decisions about their individual learning right from the start. Contextualised learning was encouraged wherever possible rather than single subject teaching and pupils developed their skills through practical sessions, for example teddy bear treasure hunts for reception classes. Staff were encouraged to experiment with the curriculum and take ownership of it, meaning that everyone played a part in its creation, generating an environment of total involvement.

A curriculum that encourages communication skills will allow plenty of time for pupils to make mistakes and to learn from them. It will also include opportunities to play with language and to share creations. Older pupils will wish to continue to develop as effective communicators if they enjoy communicating. This can only happen where teachers have time to listen and respect children as individuals with valid views and interesting things to say. Throughout life, effective communicators have good social skills, can use the right sort of 'voice' for different circumstances but also have a strong sense of their own voice, will listen and respond, will communicate successfully and will develop their thinking through the use of language, in particular with others.

Communication is not only about spoken language (and the body language which accompanies it), but also about written language. Unfortunately, the current school system prizes written language above spoken language, and puts immense pressure on children to learn to read and write at increasingly younger ages. However, before they can learn to read, children need a rich language environment and an enjoyment of books and stories. Learning to read includes learning to distinguish between sounds (phonemic awareness), matching sounds to letters (phonic awareness), fluency, vocabulary knowledge and comprehension. These skills are also important in learning to write, along with the physical skills needed to hold a pencil. In an age of increasing digital communication we should, perhaps, include here skills in visual communication, such as communication through still and moving images and the skills required to coordinate visual, spoken and written communication used on the web and other technology. For young children this is about using their own drawings, and then symbols, to communicate.

As they get older, pupils will learn to appreciate not only how to use these communication skills, but also to understand the strength of this kind of communication. Communication skills are not only about communicating with others, but also about developing an awareness of the use of communication in persuasion and manipulation.

Most descriptions of interpersonal skills are about the development of effective communication, the kind that enables positive relationships. Typologies of interpersonal skills include items such as:

- listening;
- body language;
- negotiating;
- giving and receiving criticism;
- assertiveness;
- empathy.

There is an uncertain boundary between interpersonal and intrapersonal skills. The former are about social relations, the latter are about the self, but can often be observed only in social situations. We do not wish to agonise over the difference between a skill and an attribute. In placing communication, interpersonal and intrapersonal skills together, our skills list avoids arguments of definition.

Educationists' lists of intrapersonal skills typically include items such as:

- self-knowledge and self-esteem;
- self-management, motivation and personal goal-setting;
- decision-making;
- listening;
- negotiating.

There is some replication with interpersonal skills and there are others that truly belong here, but are often treated separately, perhaps in order to emphasise their importance. These are:

- thinking skills;
- learning skills;
- skills of creativity.

We shall return to these later.

Much of the literature on interpersonal and intrapersonal skills relates to the workplace. Its constant theme is the ever increasing necessity for successful organisations to employ people with good interpersonal skills, including communication and characteristics such as the ability to adapt and change and creativity and innovation. In fact, the academic literature is clearer about the needs of employers than, say, employers' organisations, in Britain at least.

As mentioned earlier, the characteristics desired in the workplace are very similar to those contributing to success in the whole range of social roles played by people. Who could deny that the kinds of skills discussed here are crucial to success in family life? To argue that they should be central to the curriculum and assessment is not to argue for an employability curriculum. It is a recognition of what people need to negotiate every aspect of their increasingly complex, stressful and fast moving existence.

This has been widely picked up in the education world, but often the language is subtlety different. In the world of employment they talk of competencies; in education they talk of emotional literacy or emotional intelligence. The danger in adopting the language of emotional intelligence is its association with popular but academically contentious theories, such as Gardner's work on multiple intelligences. He identifies intra- and inter-personal intelligences, but no convincing case has been made for calling the associated sets of skills and qualities 'intelligences'. Curriculum agencies in this country have avoided such controversy by including personal skills within that catch-all box labelled 'personal, social and health education' (national curriculum), 'personal, social and emotional development' (foundation stage), 'social, emotional and behavioural' (Primary National Strategy) and 'personal development' (14–19).

These skills must be listed in a national curriculum. It could be argued that the PSHE curriculum does that, but the present arrangements do not meet the demand for balance. The content is found in non-statutory guidance, and within the present pressure cooker system its lack of status is confirmed by the lack of statutory assessment. The not-so-hidden message for schools is that the state does not want schools to lose focus on the core curriculum and that schools will get no league table credit for the personal development of their pupils. With the exception of a minority who remain committed to really useful education, schools have obliged. This is at odds with the statement of aims in Curriculum 2000, and very much at odds with the real needs of pupils.

Opponents of a skills-defined curriculum argue that personal skills are a good example of things that should be 'caught and not taught' in schools. In a sense, the case is that the hidden curriculum should be found, made explicit, but left informal. Personal skills can be developed through appropriate pedagogy, class and school organisation and the overall ethos of the school.

The case made in this book is that the national curriculum should include the most important outcomes for children, described as skills. The case, in this section, is that the world faces change at an unprecedented rate and this necessitates high levels of personal and interpersonal skills. Not only must these skills be listed with high priority in the national curriculum, they must also be taught explicitly and assessed explicitly. There is growing research evidence that explicit coverage produces better outcomes than reliance on the informal curriculum. A simple way of expressing this position is to propose that the PSHE curriculum is revised, expanded and given equal assessment status with other skills.

Closely linked with communication and personal skills are thinking and learning skills. According to the QCA model, thinking skills include creative thinking, enquiry, evaluation, information processing and reasoning. Children develop as thinkers from very early on as they attempt to make sense of the world in which they live. Not only do they make logical predictions based on experience, but they also begin, from about the age of three, to develop what is known as a 'theory of mind'; an understanding that others think and see the world differently. The ability to think about one's own thinking and that of others is important to learning.

Research shows that if children are given support, by the age of seven they are generally able to:

- use 'thinking language' involving words such as 'think', 'know', 'guess' and 'remember';
- construct informal rules for the purpose of solving problems;
- sort objects according to one or more criteria;
- understand that the beliefs of others may be different from their own;
- understand that because someone has partial knowledge of something they will not necessarily have all of it;
- hypothesise about what might happen in relation to future events;
- suggest alternative actions that could have been taken in the past (though this is more difficult than thinking about the future);
- reason logically from given precepts.

Recent research highlights the importance of sustained shared thinking for children's learning. It is more likely to occur when children are interacting with a single adult or peer partner and during focussed group work. The sustained shared thinking interactions include *scaffolding*, *extending*, *discussing*, *modelling* and *playing*. Research has suggested that a wide range of teaching techniques and strategies might be appropriate.

For children, then, thinking skills are about all of these: questioning, evaluating, processing information, problem solving, reflecting, ethical reasoning, balancing thought, and creative thinking.

There is a large overlap between thinking skills and learning skills. In the well known curriculum development project *Opening Minds*, led by the Royal Society of Arts, competence for learning includes understanding how to learn and to manage learning, with an emphasis on recognising learning styles, learning to think, understanding creative talents, enjoying learning, and achieving high standards in literacy, numeracy, spatial understanding and ICT. Despite the growing critique of the concept of learning styles, its widespread use in schools has had the advantage of encouraging pupils to think explicitly about how they learn.

According to the QCA reflective learners assess their skills and needs, recognise their achievements, set clear objectives with success criteria for their development and work, review progress against success criteria, invite feedback and deal positively with praise and criticism, evaluate learning and make changes to achieve success. The Campaign For Learning, in association with Guy Claxton, set out the five 'Rs' of learning: readiness, resourcefulness, resilience, remembering and reflectiveness. They believe that learning is learnable and that through learning to learn, children gain an awareness of their learning preferences and strengths. Then children can motivate themselves and develop the self-confidence to succeed. Other things to be considered include the importance of proper hydration, nutrition, sleep and a positive environment for learning. In addition, there are specific strategies that can be used to improve memory, or to make sense of complex information, or for reflecting on their learning so as to improve next time.

Bishops Park College, Essex

Located in a concentration of the most deprived wards in Essex, Bishops Park College is thriving as a result of the implementation of a curriculum reform. The headteacher believes that the school should provide a means of 'building and sustaining relationships and fostering a strong sense of belonging and mutual respect', and that a human scale, holistic curriculum be developed, encompassing the traditional means of education. Bishops Park has now developed what they call their 'tartan curriculum', which ranges from multidisciplinary work to single subject, to special interest and recreation. Learning is organised into themes, which last for one term at a time and students work with a small team of five or six teachers and support staff. Almost three and a half days per week are spent on themes. Masterclasses take place each Friday, and last all day, where a teacher can share a skill. In addition to normal after-school activities clubs run every Wednesday for a half term; well over half the students attend these clubs. Three-day faculty projects run at the end of each half term, which involves a programme of ten investigative events that aim to widen the curriculum and give students and teachers the chance to work with different groups.

The present emphasis within the curriculum and assessment system of checking the knowledge acquired makes memory skills very important. If learning is about individuals actively making sense from the environment and assimilating or accommodating that 'sense' into their world picture, then there needs to be a much more reflective aspect to learning. It is also important that learners can take control of their own learning, be self-directed and self-motivated. Learning also has a social dimension to it, including joint knowledge-construction. Then learning skills include social and communication skills, the ability to participate in dialogue and to understand the point of view of others.

Children learn best through play. Through play, children develop social skills and move from the concrete to the more abstract. Role play is particularly important, as children move from familiar roles to more imaginative play. Throughout the national curriculum years, the communication, personal, learning and thinking skills advocated here cry out for a pedagogy which makes pupils active; they require pupils to interact, try things and then reflect. Readers, ask yourselves: unless moving a pen across a piece of paper is described as active, does present practice as determined by the national curriculum and testing arrangements fit this description? Our answer: only in some places.

It was argued earlier that the second most important element in a twenty-first century education derives from the urgent need for the ability to understand and engage in the social world. Personal and communication skills lay a foundation but they focus on small scale and mainly face-to-face interaction.

Prior to the national curriculum, many secondary schools and some primary schools, developed social study courses for this purpose, but social studies was too non-traditional for the national curriculum. The 'S' in PSHE stands for social but PSHE has never been real social studies. It is the box for 'social problems', or more accurately for moral panics, which have led to demands for schools to 'do something about...' As discussed previously, it is all too tempting for politicians to see a state curriculum as the solution for such demands, and into the box has gone sex, drugs and rock'n'roll, or a close approximation thereto. More latterly, citizenship was added to the mix, but this just added to the mess. The large majority of secondary schools which did not value PSHE declined to increase the time allocation when citizenship became compulsory, and found it difficult to understand what citizenship was about. There is little doubt that David Blunkett knew what he meant when he decided to introduce it, and there is no doubt that his mentor, Bernard Crick, was clear in his own mind. But many schools have not spent the time necessary to think about what it might mean for them. Embedded deep in the sub-structure of citizenship are some important ideas which need to be considered by all pupils, but as part of a much larger set of capabilities.

Many people believe that citizenship is about schools being forced to justify government and its policies. This is mistaken. The element of citizenship which should be carried over into a skills-defined curriculum is the ability to participate in the polity. This complex of skills requires a large measure of understanding, it is true, but the understanding should equip pupils to interact with others with a sense of shared interests as members of groups from family, through community to society and the world's people. They need to be skilled in combination; this means combining with others to pursue shared interests and reacting to power exercised by others. In turn, this needs an understanding of the locations of power in our society and the world. The skill needs to be catalysed by a sense that the social world is made not by mysterious and unavoidable forces but by human beings acting collectively.

Schools that embrace citizenship tend to treat it not only as a 'subject' but also as a value that runs across school life. It must be admitted that this kind of political skill is dangerous for schools; in developing pupils' skills to challenge power, schools are laying themselves open to challenge, and it is a useful lesson for pupils to realise that very few schools see themselves as democratic institutions and very few people think they ought to be. Pupil voice, an important element in a reflexive pedagogy, is not the same thing as pupil vote.

It would be too limited for pupils to focus only on their own schools as case studies for the development of political skills. They need to be outward looking. This may start with their own community and learning how to make things happen at local level, but should move on to the national and international levels. Many schools are now using ICT to build relationships with schools across the world, and can develop combinations at that level. As well as combining with people who are obviously like themselves, pupils need to develop the ability to see commonalities of experience and interest with those who are not obviously like themselves. As Britain becomes a main global migration hub this is necessary at local, national, and international levels.

Eventually, we arrive at academic skills. Are they towards the end of the list because they matter less? No, they are preceded in this chapter by physical, personal, creative, thinking, learning and political skills for emphasis. It is to say that *this* is the logical makeup of a broad and balanced curriculum. *This* is what parity of esteem would really look like. *This* is a comprehensive curriculum for the twenty-first century, one which meets the learning needs of all our children and young people of compulsory school age.

We propose that national curriculum designers learn from and replicate the work we see taking place, quietly, in schools across the country, particularly primary schools. Teachers are taking national curriculum subjects and extracting from them the skills required in each and bringing them together to provide a unified learning experience. Although this comes naturally to generalist primary school teachers, the new key stage 3 national curriculum explicitly encourages this kind of development in secondary schools also.

It might be thought that some secondary school teachers who are deeply committed to their subjects would resist the development of a rebalanced national curriculum, which apparently relegates academic subjects. We know that love of subject is a strong motivation for some people to join the profession and they should not gain the impression that these proposals are an attack on their professionalism. On the contrary, they would enjoy the opportunity to think through anew the rationale for their disciplines in contributing to the national debate on the skills curriculum. The removal of knowledge content from the national curriculum would also enhance their professionalism, by giving them the responsibility to determine which aspects of their subject are most deserving of coverage by their pupils.

At heart those teachers who are subject enthusiasts long most to transfer to their pupils their enthusiasm and understanding of their subject. They know that this is not achieved by pupils memorising 'facts' for a test, but through active learning experiences that transmit the essence of the subject. To return to an earlier example, the young historian is not a pupil who spends a long time learning a string of historic dates. The young historian understands chronology and enjoys the idea of locating evidence, weighing pieces of evidence, having regard to their sources, and coming to judgments about past events. History is an example of a subject already partly defined in terms of skills such as these, and its assessment attempts to be consistent with this. The skills-based curriculum simply extends the idea by promoting this approach to all subjects.

It is possible that a skills-mapping exercise would reveal that some academic skills are developed in a number of subjects, and decisions about rationalising their delivery might be indicated. The virtue of the skills-based curriculum is that it would be for schools to decide how to organise their time to ensure coverage of all the skills, including the academic.

Hook CE Primary School, Yorkshire

At Hook CE Primary School the headteacher aims to 'develop lively, enquiring, imaginative and creative minds, and for children to have the ability to question and argue rationally and to apply themselves to tasks'. Hence, they have successfully developed a curriculum model that encourages children to work from their own first hand experience, which develops their interest and motivates them, giving them a sense of relevance and purpose in their work. The school uses a cross-curricular thematic approach in their planning. Off school site visits take place at the beginning of each term, which then set the theme for the rest of the term. Pupils' independence is strongly encouraged at all stages and they are able to comment on teachers' planning and carry out their own assessments. The school does not work to a timetable which allows the flexibility to work on a project for an extended period.

We are not attempting to write a definitive list of skills. We are not analysing every subject vying for space on the curriculum for their relevance and essential skills. Neither do we assume that the fresh start approach we call for will produce only those skills connected with the present common school subjects. The national debate we hope for will stimulate proponents of a range of disciplines to market their wares. One example that springs to mind is the claim that ethics should be on the timetable for all, bringing together various areas of the curriculum where the moral dimension to humanity currently appear.

This is our last word in support of skills as the basis for curriculum design. Is it the last word? We hope not, we expect to provoke debate and opposition. If we start from a consensus that the curriculum we have is not what we need, then we hope the way forward suggested in this chapter will be compared with other suggestions.

In the following two chapters, we discuss how the knowledge aspects of the curriculum should be designed within the skills framework, and then the thorny issue of how this kind of curriculum might be assessed.

CHAPTER FIVE

Local knowledge

As we saw earlier, although understanding and skill are not the same thing, the boundary between them is indistinct. In practice it is impossible to develop a skill without gaining knowledge or understanding. We have explained why the state does not need to describe the whole curriculum, why it is important to specify the skills it wants to see every child develop and why it does not need to specify the knowledge content.

In this chapter we look again at knowledge and understanding, and make the case for local determination of what should be taught. Some difficulties are intrinsic to a state curriculum defined in terms of knowledge, which is essentially the current experience of the English model. As we have seen, a national curriculum is necessarily an inflexible document. It is the result of a substantial bureaucratic effort, a process in which debating, drafting and consulting are reiterative until the final Parliamentary approval is given, after which alteration seems a task too far.

Since the introduction in 1989 of the original programmes of study for the national curriculum subjects, there has been some change, as described in Chapter 3. Although ministerial interference accounts for some of it, other changes have been initiated by educationists, led by the QCA and its predecessors in response to professional opinion. The fact remains that there is widespread dissatisfaction amongst the profession with the current curriculum.

For conservatives, it is not a problem that a state curriculum is slow to change. Some people think that the body of knowledge to be transmitted should be universal and timeless and most teachers would readily concede that though some items have been taught for decades they should probably continue to be. Few teachers, if any, however, would say that this applies to all items on the list.

Unfortunately, the world is not helping this ultra-conservative position. In every sphere of human intellectual endeavour, the volume of production is increasing as never before. So is the rate of production. It is true that fewer than two people read an average doctorate thesis, much of this new knowledge does not change the paradigm. On the other hand, a tiny proportion of it does. Few fiction readers, for example, would contest either of the propositions that most of the classical canon of the novel remains worthy of both reading and study, and that the best modern novelists move forward our understanding of what can be achieved by this genre. As the total knowledge of our physical and social worlds doubles and redoubles, the onus on educators is continually to re-assess the selection of that knowledge to ensure it is worthy of transmission.

'In times of change learners inherit the earth while the learned find themselves beautifully equipped for a world that no longer exists.'
Eric Hoffer, philosopher.

A simple example of this is the change in the number of planets in the solar system, which occurred in 2006. Now it is true that the national curriculum does not stipulate how many planets there are in the Solar System and teachers can easily replace nine with eight, but the re-designation of Pluto does change the popular understanding of the criteria required to qualify as a planet, and this ought to be reflected within the curriculum.

The frequency of a fact no longer being a fact, however, is a less common feature of the knowledge explosion. More common is the accretion of additional facts, or new hypotheses, theories, or understandings, to an existing body of knowledge. Each item on its own may be unworthy of specific reference in a national curriculum, but their cumulative effect might be such that they lead to a revised understanding of a specific subject area. As stated before, the challenge for the teacher in dealing with the explosion is to ensure that what is selected is worthwhile. There are some areas of learning where this is particularly important and especially difficult; social and political studies and science are subject to rapid change with huge consequence to society. In these areas in particular, there is a strong argument that change is too rapid for a state curriculum to keep up. What learners and teachers need is a more flexible arrangement to enable them to respond quickly to a changing knowledge base.

One line of argument for a stable curriculum is linked to the idea of 'national heritage'. It emphasises the role of schools to transmit to succeeding generations an understanding of the best of the nation's achievements in the course of socialising the young into what it is to be... well, probably, English, though often described as British. Many teachers would no doubt agree that this is part of their role, but proper consideration reveals serious difficulties with this position.

Firstly, in most areas of knowledge, there can be no equivalence between nationality and 'the best that has been thought or known'. Using this criterion, we would expect the educated person to know of Tolstoy as well as Shakespeare. In practice, heritage is supposed to mean ensuring the achievements of Britons in any given field are given prominence, and that Britain's achievements are emphasised in school history. It is also worth noting that most supporters of this position expect heritage to be transmitted informally through the hidden curriculum too, although they are not explicit about this; they may speak of fair play being learnt through the pastoral and disciplinary systems.

Secondly, one difficulty here is the tendency to make this point from an anglocentric, or even metropolitan, perspective. Despite some recent popular debate, there is a lack of clarity about what we in the UK mean by nationality. The propensity of many but not all Scots to support any opponent of England in a sporting competition is not without significance; few supporters of the 'national heritage' idea put Burns alongside Wordsworth. And as for the Britishness of Northern Ireland, well…

Thirdly, it's not just geography that puts the idea of 'national heritage' in doubt. Many people who talk about it really mean what is often called 'high culture', which in reality is closely related to the lifestyle of an upper class which asserts the right to define quality. If we use the sociological meaning of culture, the shared, persistent, and transmitted lifestyle of a group in a complex society like modern Britain, then there are many cultures. High culture is distinctive and not shared by other social classes; class cultures remain strong and differentiated. Class, however, is only one factor that differentiates the English. There remain, more strongly towards the geographical margins, regional cultures. When the metropolitan, urban and rural factors are overlaid, we find a complex pattern of lifestyles with mutual, and sometimes antagonistic, recognition of difference. Urban dwellers seek to consume cheap food; rural dwellers need high prices for agricultural products.

In addition to class and region, there is an argument for the existence of gender cultures. Men and women in our society continue to have different life experiences. There has also long been a common assumption of the existence of a youth culture. Lastly, of course, the cultural map of Britain is now changing ever more rapidly as global migration becomes a marked feature of the new century.

So a brief glance at contemporary British society reveals a complexity which defeats any attempt to define the national heritage, or a 'British way of life'. For many centuries England has been an importer not just of goods but also of people, language, beliefs and customs. This leads us to the final argument against basing a national curriculum on an idea of transmitting a national culture: the pace of social and cultural change in contemporary society. Many adherents of the national heritage idea place great stress on British history; for example, the values of democracy as it was established in the revolutions of the seventeenth century. However, the present concern with so-called global terrorism illustrates that in this century people in Britain will have a much greater need to understand the history and politics of the world struggle for control of energy and water, and of the global responses to empires, in order to prevent catastrophes in their lives.

To argue against basing a curriculum on a 'British heritage' with an unchanging body of important knowledge is not anti-British. It just reflects the classrooms that teachers occupy: where children learn to use new technologies before their teachers do, where children come from worlds very different from those experienced by the metropolitan middle class, and where Britishness is redefined daily. The problem of how to select what today's youngsters need from the explosively expanding volume of knowledge cannot be solved by reference to any version of a classical education thought appropriate for a privileged class now long since past. What's more, what looks to teachers like the right selection varies hugely because so does the make-up and the needs of their pupils.

There is a further difficulty created by a national curriculum with an overloaded knowledge specification. It appears to pupils as an imposition. The knowledge is external to them, and because it is not determined with them in mind it seems to be not for them. As we saw earlier, research suggests that the best learning occurs when pupils co-create their own knowledge. We need, as they say, learners to own the knowledge they gain. As we shall see later, they don't at the moment. They forget quicker than you can say, 'It's time for re-test'.

However, few teachers would stretch that argument to the conclusion that pupils themselves should plan the knowledge aspect of their learning. Their sense of ownership comes from a starting point provided by their teachers to an end point probably reached collaboratively. School pupils by definition are not mature adults, and even mature adults often need help in identifying their own learning needs, so it would not be safe to allow pupils to determine knowledge content without guidance and support from their teachers.

The question remains: who is to decide what knowledge should be contained in the curriculum? Neither end of the spectrum, the state nor the pupil, is in a sound position to make this decision. The obvious conclusion to draw then is that teachers should select it locally.

Why is selection by teachers the obvious solution? Because they are the right people in the right place. They have the necessary professional skills. Those who were educated some time ago, as opposed to those trained recently, have studied the philosophy of education and know something about the principles of curriculum design. They are very familiar with the content of the present curriculum, either the key stage (primary) or subject (secondary). Teachers also have experience that will enable them to apply their previous understanding to the circumstances of their schools. They have received feedback from their pupils amounting to a critique of the present curriculum. They will be able to reflect on what would better suit the pupils they teach, although some will need prompting because this practice has slipped out of the culture of teaching under the imposition of a total curriculum.

One significant problem with this approach is: how are pupils to be assessed if they are not learning standard items? This issue is addressed in Chapter 6.

'Selection by teachers' could mean lots of different things in practice. It could refer, at one end of the spectrum, to completely independent decisions by individual teachers for their classes alone. At the other end, it could mean a national model devised by teachers' representatives. The argument above must imply a degree of independence for individual teachers, to enable them to tailor pupils' learning to their needs, but in today's circumstances this is constrained. Not only would a school expect to have a curriculum policy, there would also need to be external accountability.

What would make one local curriculum different from another? It would contain knowledge of specific relevance to the community. Communities vary according to all the categories discussed earlier. Their cultures reflect class, region, religion, gender and migration effects, and may change rapidly with their circumstances. The curricula offered by their schools should reflect these variations and be responsive to change. If teachers are to be responsible for deciding which items of local culture should be included in the knowledge component of the curriculum, they need a relationship with the community to guide them and to endorse their decisions.

To place this responsibility with teachers is the logical conclusion to the popular argument that public services are better if local decisions are made by the appropriate professionals. No one questions the responsibility of medical staff to decide patient treatment within their own areas of competence. On the other hand, teachers lost that right in 1988 precisely because the country felt it could no longer trust them.

No matter how much or little the Government feels it can trust teachers, they must be accountable. That much is generally agreed. The current mechanism with respect to the curriculum is that OfSTED reports on the quality of a school's curriculum, including its compliance, or otherwise, with the national curriculum. In theory, OfSTED could continue to report on compliance with a skills-based national curriculum and a locally determined knowledge content, but this would be much more complex and difficult to standardise. Neither would it meet the need for local accountability for a local curriculum.

It must be said that what that accountability should look like in itself requires a debate within the education community at national and local levels. It may be that already existing mechanisms can be turned to such use, but it may be that new mechanisms will be required. A question that requires early answer is how will the community be defined for this purpose?

At the moment, years of implementation of policies designed to create and sustain quasi-markets for schools have emphasised the relationship between a school and its parents (including carers), and perhaps its potential parents, and de-emphasised its relationship with the community as a whole. This has been accompanied by an undue focus on the school's purpose with respect to the achievement of individual pupils (but narrowly defined at that) to the neglect of the school's important social purposes.

While of course many teachers have been seduced by the

standards agenda, or forced into compliance by pressure from league tables or OfSTED, the profession as a whole remains committed to a British perspective on the purposes of schooling. This includes a collective purpose, involving links with the local community. These take many forms, from allowing community groups to use the school accommodation to supporting local action groups by way of helping mums with official forms. Recent thinking on community emphasises the importance for community identity. It is easier for a school to conceive itself as a community resource if it can identify with a specific place, and most primary schools are in that position, together with some secondary schools. Those secondary schools that attract pupils from a very large catchment area are unlikely to value a community support role, however.

This working relationship between a school and its community may be lasting, or may be dependent on key people who move on eventually. Only rarely is it used for a real review of the school's curriculum. In recent years there have been requirements for schools to consult parents about curriculum areas, notably on sex and relationships and drugs education, but 'parents' cannot be taken as a proxy for 'community'. Parents' interest in a school is transitory, the more so in days of small families and geographical mobility. Parents are also notorious for an interest in their child alone, rather than the school as a whole, even a proportion of those who volunteer to govern the school do so out of limited interest. Although recent governments have seemed unable to comprehend this, the limited concern of parents puts them in a different interest group from that of communities. Parents would always want the best for their school, regardless of other schools. They would prefer their school to be the highest funded rather than fairly funded. They would always fight to keep their school open, rather than support a necessary rationalisation. Decisions about what is taught in schools affect everyone, not just the parents of the moment. If there is to be local accountability for the knowledge aspects of the curriculum it cannot be expressed only or mainly through parents.

The problem remains, how can it be expressed? There is a simple answer. Within our constitution, the local council is the representative of the local community. It is elected and accountable to the community. If our constitution works, the local council ought to be capable of working with schools to ensure that their curricula meet their area's needs. This thought however, produces complications of its own. In England, there is what might be called a 'rich and varied pattern of local government'. We have the London boroughs, the metropolitan boroughs, the unitary authorities, the district councils and the county councils. The cities are fragmented, and their boundaries do not always coincide with recognised community maps, but their council areas are small enough to allow genuine community involvement, and there are LAs for education. In rural areas district councils have real local connection but do not have responsibility for education, while the county councils that do may find it difficult to keep tabs on their schools in these autonomous times. And as always, administrative reform is in the air, currently with the Lyons review. There may well be a case for a more regional dimension to curriculum decisions. So the question remains, if the community interest in curriculum can best be expressed through existing local democratic bodies, which tier of local government is best placed to carry out this function? Educationists should seek to inject this question into the current round of debate regarding the future of local government.

But there may be a less simple answer that would work better. Is there a case for the establishment of bodies for the single purpose of linking schools and communities on curriculum matters? The assumption behind the local council model is that each one takes responsibility for a number of schools; hundreds in the shire council case, but a purpose built model might be designed on a one per school model, or perhaps one per place, where a place is a recognisable community. On the face of it, this seems likely to be unduly complicated, although it would have one virtue. Most groups and activists who support communities work on a similar scale. It would have the scope to provide direct access to schools for them, rather than indirectly through the councillor.

Lastly the argument could be made that this small scale accountability mechanism already exists in the form of the governing body. It already has curriculum responsibilities. Unfortunately, no one outside a small group of enthusiasts believes that governing bodies as presently constituted generally provide a genuine community accountability.

So there is a challenge for those of us who believe in the local curriculum, with decisions made by teachers. It must be the case that the decisions must be open to local scrutiny. The debate must be how that scrutiny can be ordered in such a way as to give the community an opportunity to influence proposals and to endorse decisions, but not for counter-productive interference in day-to-day working. It is not the biggest issue in the adoption of a new curriculum model, but it is an important detail that will require a solution.

We now turn to the question of what the knowledge content of the new curriculum might be. The short answer is that it is not for us to say. The argument is precisely that teachers, in their own circumstances, should make that decision. However, it might be helpful to speculate on what decisions they might make.

The assertion made earlier that the concept of a national culture is problematic should not mask the reality that when the education community is invited to contribute to curriculum design, there are large areas of general agreement. As noted in Chapter 3, the original national curriculum was introduced on a wave of consensus, in which a strong view of what a broad and balanced curriculum should contain was developed. History suggests, then, that teachers are likely to produce similar answers, with specific differences arising from the circumstances of the communities they work in.

This scenario will not be acceptable to all. Some politicians want the certainty that 'Britishness' will be transmitted, particularly through knowledge of British history. The debate about this is a good illustration of the principle that all curriculum decisions are political, since the relative importance of national identity in the twenty-first century world is essentially a political question. We are arguing essentially for devolution of political decision making to schools, under the oversight of the local community. It will be for teachers to judge whether their pupils need to understand more about Britain's past, or more how the world as a whole came to be in its present state. To deny teachers that judgement is to mistake their place in society and misread their professionalism. It is true, as claimed sometimes, that there could be no certainty that every pupil would be taught about the Battle of Trafalgar, but is there any reason to assume that history teachers would consider it too unimportant to cover? And given the way the world has gone since the history curriculum was agreed by Parliament, should not history teachers be given the opportunity to consider the balance of importance of the Napoleonic wars against, say, the Opium wars?

And maybe, a little more emphasis on both global and local citizenship in our schools and a little less on the importance of Britishness would be a contribution to a tolerant society with good community relations.

In a locally determined curriculum, then, much of the knowledge content is likely to be similar to that of the current national curriculum, certainly at first. Teachers are likely to select from the knowledge currently specified, and alter the emphasis between the items selected according to local circumstances.

Over time, this democratisation of knowledge is likely to lead to a greater variety of knowledge learnt. As schools and pupils focus more on learning and thinking skills they will adjust to pupils contributing to their own learning as researchers and collaborators in producing knowledge. Whatever the Government's slogan 'personalised learning' really means, if anything, taking knowledge out of the national curriculum will permit pupils, perhaps individually, but more likely in small groups or whole classes, to acquire the knowledge they want and need. Since none of us can expect to know more than a tiny and decreasing proportion of all that is known in the world, and none of us know the same as our neighbour, does it matter if school leavers do not all know the same things? Does it matter if this group of youngsters read this novel and that group read that novel? Wouldn't it be great if youngsters read a novel!? If a local curriculum with an active and engaging pedagogy replaces the present (too often literally) depressing diet, pupil engagement will increase and so will the total amount of knowledge learnt.

It should be remembered that the variety of knowledge would be within a framework of a broad and balanced curriculum. This would be ensured by including key subject skills within the national curriculum. For example, the skills of scientific enquiry would have to be learnt through a body of scientific knowledge, although science would become more practical as the assessment of skills requires an active pedagogy. Science is one subject where practitioners have been conducting a debate about content, with the new GCSE syllabus the latest response. Presumably, there will be local innovation reflecting the views expressed in this debate, and the science teaching community will accumulate evidence on what works best.

Stimulating local innovation is one of the most important aims of this curriculum design. As shown elsewhere, it is the tradition of teachers in this country to develop their own curricula. In a period where school improvement is a multi-million business, no one could deny that a renewed power to innovate in classrooms is a circuit of a spiral, not a circle. No structural innovation would be needed in order to promote the best solutions; the QCA and TeacherNet, to name but two, are already in the business. When innovation becomes the norm rather than the exception the only challenge would be to catalogue the material. As to checking poor practice, the profession is now scarcely short of accountability mechanisms.

Before moving on to consider the changes that might take place in the types of knowledge learnt the effects of the skills curriculum on the organisation of learning needs to be considered. A common but not universal factor in schools that have tried to develop a skills curriculum has been to revise the timetable. This question is likely to be addressed differently in primary schools than in secondary schools. Much of the current bottom-up curriculum innovation is found in primary schools, which are better equipped to evaluate the overall learning experiences of pupils. Although they are now required (implicitly, by the National Strategy) to devote undue time to dedicated English and maths lessons many would prefer to return to a more fluid organisation of the school day. Some of the case studies in this book illustrate how the school day might be loosened up so that the pursuit of interesting learning experiences are not artificially halted by the bell.

In secondary schools there is more varied opinion on whether the current standard subject timetable arrangements meet pupils' needs. Teachers of some subjects prefer little and often, others want long enough to allow completion of a more extended task. Many schools have introduced longer timetable blocks to limit year 7 movement, or to reduce the insecurity of more needy pupils; innovation in the organisation of the school day is commonplace in secondary schools. If curriculum design were handed over to teachers there would certainly be renewed debate, but such change is not inevitable and where teachers remain strongly committed to the subject ethos it would perhaps not be wise to make changes in the first instance. As we saw at Govan High School a skills-based curriculum was introduced without timetable change, partly in order to reassure staff that their subjects were still seen as important.

Further speculation about possible future trends in the organisation of lessons has been sparked by the continuing debate on 'personalisation'. All versions of future models of teaching and learning assume a much larger place for IT as a learning tool. It ought to be obvious that the possibilities for innovation in pedagogy, including but not only by means of the use of new technologies, are constrained by a system of universal tests of knowledge defined by the national curriculum. A major advantage of local determination of knowledge content is precisely that it would enable the curriculum and pedagogy to be developed together at school level. One result of this freedom would be experimentation with the organisation of learning. As long as innovations are evaluated, with the promotion of the successful and the relegation of the unsuccessful, this can only add strength to the system as a whole.

A central proposition within this book is that decentralised responsibility for the knowledge aspect of the curriculum would increase the vibrancy and development of the school system. It would lead to an increase in the national stock of skill and understanding about the curriculum, pedagogy and assessment. So it cannot be for this book to propose what knowledge should be contained in the curriculum. We do not intend to try to second-guess the collective skill of the nation's teachers, and indeed the point is that we would expect teachers in different situations to produce different curriculum designs. There is no list here of the items of knowledge we would expect to see.

If the national curriculum is limited to a statement of essential skills, the knowledge content of the curriculum can be determined locally. In this chapter, we argue how this would produce learning more responsive to the varying needs of pupils and a fast changing world. We recognise that if teachers are given this responsibility they must be accountable locally for their decisions, and point out the need for a debate as to how this might work. We also suggest that at first there would not be a radical change in what is taught, and we may expect evolution as teachers come to terms with their new autonomy. Over the next two chapters, we examine some implications of this structure. In Chapter 7, we discuss the impact on teachers, but first we look at the changes that would be necessary to the way pupils are assessed.

Assessing the skills curriculum

Assessment is a crucial part of curriculum and of learning. It has been defined as, 'what we do when we take stock of how a learner is progressing'[1]. Before outlining the type of assessment needed to complement a skills-defined curriculum, let's look at the elements of the current assessment system in England and its effects on the curriculum as presently taught within schools. These effects, often caused by the choices available or the lack of them around method ('how') and purpose ('why'), have been a strong motivation for reform.

Currently pupils experience years of national assessment and testing; if you count baseline assessment most pupils who go on to take 'A' Levels will have undergone national assessments and tests in 10 of their 13 years of schooling. Yet prior to 1988, pupils faced only two external national tests at 16+ and 18+, with a minority taking the 11+. The Government has tried to use the test system for a plethora of purposes, and this bedevils it.

While the concept of summative assessment may be simple, the uses of data from summative assessment are varied and the requirements of different uses make varying demands in relation to reliability and validity of the assessment'[2].

Research by the QCA has listed no fewer than 18 different uses for test results, including system monitoring, school choice and selection[3]. It has been argued that even a well-constructed test is not valid if the results are used inappropriately. This moves the idea of validity on from something which is the concern of test writers to something which is the responsibility of all who interpret and use assessment results[1].

In other countries national monitoring needs are met through a system of regular surveys of small random samples of pupils, thus reducing the overall test burden whilst increasing the relevance and breadth of the learner evidence. In the US the National Assessment of Educational Progress is used, in New Zealand the National Education Monitoring Project, and nearer to home in Scotland, the Scottish Survey of Achievement. However, none of these programmes produce the school level data apparently required for a marketised system.

In schools, the introduction of league tables of school exam and national test results has encouraged a risk-averse culture. They have encouraged 'teaching to the test' by teachers and the regurgitation by learners of key 'facts'. Teachers will always teach to the test. Indeed, in the recent past ministers have made a virtue of this, arguing that pupils have an entitlement to knowledge and that the tests check whether the entitlement has been delivered. However, the pressure to do so has never been greater. There is much evidence that teachers pick questions, provide model answers, repeatedly coach in narrow areas of performance. Just one year after the introduction of an on-line test of key stage 3 IT, teachers were anticipating which areas of the syllabus were amenable to on-line testing and skewing their teaching and test preparation accordingly. The system has created an imbalance between professional autonomy, professional judgement and accountability.

This enhances the likelihood that pupils will learn what is often referred to as 'surface' or 'shallow learning'. This means that they are taught to recall information in a test without necessarily understanding the material. They may not be able to process the information, use it in other contexts or relate it to other information. Knowledge with understanding, or 'deep learning', where active learners have absorbed the knowledge into their own understandings of the world, is far more useful but more difficult to assess. The format of the national tests, which are written tests of limited duration, makes it impossible to assess many of the higher-level cognitive and communication skills and the ability to learn both independently and collaboratively[4].

There is strong evidence that rising test scores are not caused by rising standards of achievement but are rather the effect of growing familiarity amongst teachers and students with test requirements; research shows that changes in the tests are accompanied by a sudden fall in achievement, followed by a rise as teachers begin 'teaching to the new test[5]. Researchers have also argued that the idea of measuring standards over time in any real sense is 'nonsense' and that while reported standards are rising, the actual level of achievement could be falling; tests are no longer an adequate measure of achievement across the subject[6].

Furthermore, there is a danger that we fail to appreciate the impact of test unreliability. Proponents for exams cite their supposed objectivity, but public examination grades are not exact measures; they are approximate with known margins for error. These grades depend upon the judgement of the examiners, who whilst they are often highly professional, skilled and experienced individuals they are also fallible human beings. Although they are particularly concerned with reliability, it is likely that the proportion of students receiving an inaccurate grade due to test unreliability is at least 30% at key stage 2 and as high as 40% at key stage 3[6]. Incidentally, e-assessment will not improve the accuracy of the test scores, it may bring many advantages of efficiency but it cannot miraculously eliminate grade uncertainty.

As noted earlier, a central motivation for the introduction of the national curriculum was the entitlement of pupils to a broad and balanced curriculum. However, the testing system has had a well-documented narrowing effect on the curriculum, undermining this entitlement for many pupils, particularly in schools fearful of low scores on the league tables. In primary schools teachers' attention has been focused on literacy, numeracy and science to the detriment of the rest of the primary curriculum[7]. OfSTED stated in its 2005 evaluation of the impact of the Primary National Strategy that the standards agenda has been the primary concern of most headteachers and subject leaders, leading to a cautionary approach in promoting greater flexibility within the curriculum. OfSTED also recognised the narrowing effect which key stage 2 tests have on teaching of the curriculum and the disproportionate attention devoted to year 6 in comparison with earlier year groups[8].

An advantage of the current assessment system is said to be a large amount of data on pupil attainment and school performance, but its unreliability makes its utility doubtful. The Daugherty Assessment Review Group in Wales, reviewing assessment arrangements at key stages 2 and 3, considered whether the 'hard data… on pupil attainments and the targets it gives some pupils to aspire to, is of sufficient value to compensate for the evident impoverishment of pupils' learning that is occurring at a critical stage in their educational development'[9]. The Group didn't believe so and recommended to the Welsh Assembly that statutory national curriculum testing of 11 year-olds at key stage 2 and 14 year-olds at key stage 3 should be discontinued.

Research, ironically commissioned by the DfES, notes the lack of evidence to show that pupils reaching Level 4 at key stage 2 will retain their learning, let alone progress to higher learning. It describes how a 'level focus' and booster classes temporarily raised pupils to mathematics level 4 but that this level of progress was not sustained six months to a year after the test. Not only were learning outcomes not sustained but the research also details how high stakes assessment encouraged a more rigid teaching style which disadvantaged and lowered the self-esteem of those who prefer more active and creative ways of learning[10].

Experience teaches secondary schools that key stage 2 test results are not reliable guides to the achievement of incoming pupils; they are of little use as assessment for learning. In fact, many secondary schools carry out their own testing of year 7 pupils in the autumn term, a considerable duplication of time and effort when pupils have already been assessed in most aspects of the core subjects at the end of key stage 2[11]. It was also one of the main findings of the 2002 PPI survey, commissioned by ACCAC, that secondary schools did not make extensive use of the statutory assessment data available to them[9].

And what effect does this system have on our pupils? Pupils have become very utilitarian in their views of what is worthwhile pursuing; they have a strategic and cynical compliance with assessment requirements where passing tests is their primary focus and the concept and practice of learning is marginalised and takes second place[12]. But for lower-achieving pupils we know that the experience of frequently failing tests is demoralising and reduces their self-esteem, including their belief in their ability to succeed with other tasks[7]. Thus, the gap between higher and lower achieving pupils widens, exacerbated by the fact that focus on test outcomes reduces the levels of early identification of under-achievement and appropriate interventions as noted by OfTSED in relation to the impact of key stage 2 testing[8].

Not only are the principles of a broad and balanced curriculum undermined, so too is the current *Every Child Matters* agenda. The group of assessment experts, academics and researchers who comprise the Assessment Reform Group have also noted the lack of correlation between the narrow range of learning outcomes which are assessed by tests and the broad view of learning goals reflected in the DfES' *Every Child Matters* policy[4]. There is an ongoing tension at school level between narrow standards and broader school goals of engendering pupil enjoyment and creativity.

There are deeper problems for pupils' self-image built into the testing arrangements. Researchers have observed that pupils have varying views of the nature of ability and those views have a profound impact on how they react to challenging tasks. This reflects the philosophically problematic nature of the concept of 'ability', and in particular the concept of the 'level of ability' at a given moment. Students who see ability as a fixed entity, 'how clever you are is how clever you stay', will tackle a challenging task if they believe their chance of success is high but will not engage with it if they believe that their chance of success is low. Others, who see ability as incremental will see a challenging task as offering a chance to 'become cleverer'. But a bureaucratic system of age-dependent levels leads to a situation in which many students get the same level at ages seven, 11 and 14, thus potentially reinforcing a belief in ability as being fixed, with consequential demotivation and disengagement[6].

This testing system forces teachers to focus very largely on summative assessment, the purpose of which is to judge a student's performance at a given point of time. It discourages them from giving sufficient attention to formative assessment, the process where progress is assessed to inform further learning, and can be used to teach learners about the learning process itself and how they can become partners in their own learning. Any particular test level or grade gives no specific information about a pupil's performance. Much more information is needed if teachers in the next year group or school are to build upon pupils' prior attainment[1].

Teachers in Scotland have been supported in using formative assessment by the Assessment is for Learning (AIFL) programme, which has not led to any loss of accountability in the system. HMI produce full reports on schools, based around a set of 33 quality indicators in seven key areas, and the system strongly encourages schools to continually self-evaluate and assess achievements using these quality indicators. The AIFL programme is to be fully integrated into the national assessment system. In England, Assessment for Learning (AFL) still appears to be a separate strand from the national testing system, rather than an integrated part of a coherent whole.

In Scotland, tests have been reconfigured to make testing more manageable within the school system and less likely to distort teaching and learning. Teachers have been provided with an online bank of assessment materials based on the Scottish Survey of Achievement. The aim of these tests is to confirm teachers' assessments of their pupils' attainment. They are administered to pupils when teachers deem they are ready to take them, rather than on a pre-determined occasion.

Many observers of these programmes have made criticisms similar to the present arrangements. The curriculum model proposed here raises a number of other problems for a national assessment system. The remainder of this chapter considers what would and wouldn't work if such a curriculum were to be introduced.

The proposed model requires an assessment system which focuses learners on learning rather than tests, maintains the breadth of vision of the national curriculum that encapsulates *Every Child Matters* and engages learners as participants in their learning and progress. To spell out the logical implication of the model, if the knowledge is locally determined it cannot be tested nationally. If there are to be national tests they must relate to the national curriculum, and therefore consist of skills tests.

How can skills be tested? Exam designers have grappled with that question for many years, and some skills are amenable to written or screen assessment. The skills of scientific method, or of historical enquiry, or of thinking and learnacy, can possibly be displayed in these ways. The problem for examiners, however, is that many of the skills proposed here for inclusion in the national curriculum cannot. How can we assess the capability of a pupil as a team player, or as a leader? How can we judge their skill in using a spade or a screwdriver? How can we score their ability to adopt a variety of walking and cycling styles? The simple fact is that skills are best assessed by directly observing their performance. The logical conclusion is that the achievement of school leavers should be assessed through teacher observation of the national curriculum skills exhibited in practice.

'As an employer I am proud that my company has never required any qualification in any job we have recruited for in the past 15 years. Our principle is 'hire for attitude, train for skill'. We look for ability to work in a team, social skills, emotional intelligence and judgment in real-life situations. I am not aware of any qualication that recognises or even encourages these aspects. Instead they seem to focus on individual achievement and one narrow aspect of intelligence.'

(extract of letter to a national newspaper from the Chief Executive of Happy Computers)

This may be logical, but it may not be acceptable at first glance to many. In the following pages, the objections to the proposal are examined in detail. The first is the claim that assessment by teachers cannot be as valid or reliable as written exams. There are widespread assumptions that on the one hand tests *are* valid and reliable and that on the other teachers' assessments are unreliable and subject to bias, despite their use in some countries as a main feature of national and state systems.

Earlier in the chapter the weakness of the first assumption was exposed.

Moreover, the supposed unreliability of teacher assessment can be addressed through provision of training around identification and understanding of the assessment criteria by teachers and through training that highlights sources of potential bias[13]. Studies in Australia have shown that finer specification of criteria, describing progressive levels of competency, can lead to increased reliability of teacher assessment which uses evidence drawn from the full range of classroom activity.

Much of the evidence for bias in teachers' assessment comes mainly from studies where it is compared with a different measure. The assumption is made that the benchmark measure is unbiased and measures the same thing as the teachers' assessment. So, whilst it has been reported that teachers under-rate boys more than girls in mathematics and science, as compared with their performance in tests, the conclusion might equally be that boys perform above expectation on mathematics and science tests[5]. Some researchers have concluded that teacher assessment is prone to bias due to systematic variations between it and standards task/test performance judgements, based on the assumption that the latter measures are unbiased. Yet bias in terms of gender, first language and SEN has also been found in the results of these standard tasks and tests so their original conclusion must be called into question.

However, bias and its effects must be a key part of training for teachers so that non-relevant assessment factors such as pupil behaviour and gender are recognised as potential sources of bias and influence and are guarded against by teachers and moderators. The bias of unfamiliar situations is a risk in national standard tasks and tests, a risk that is reduced by teacher assessment at local level.

A skills curriculum encourages pupils to perform and achieve through a range of tasks, from traditional short piece writing, to multi-media projects, from demonstrating tool use to artefact construction, from group-work through to individual submissions. A range of assessment tasks involving a variety of contexts, using a range of methods and a range of response formats, is most likely to offer pupils equitable opportunity for achievement by offering them an alternative should any one type of assessment be disadvantageous to them.

For a pupil to do their best in any assessment task, it must be concrete and within the experience of the pupil (an equal access issue) and presented clearly so that the pupil can understand what is required. It also needs to be relevant to the current concerns of the pupil (to engender motivation and engagement) and set in non-threatening conditions. If assessment is under the teachers' control, they can help to ensure that these factors are present, thus making teacher assessment more equitable and thereby providing each pupil with the opportunity to achieve to the best of their ability[14].

Teachers can develop the assessment criteria, share them with learners and work with them towards the learning goals, offer feedback aimed towards improvement throughout the process and then assess against these criteria. We know that teachers are better assessors when they are part of the assessment process throughout its development. Teachers are best-placed to be local assessors, becoming expert within training, support and experience, and with accountability through a rigorous moderation process.

This model also caters for the diversity of cultures within our society. Current curriculum and assessment models are based on the idea of homogeneous knowledge owned by all. Yet even the current curriculum contains statements and intentions for the recognition of diverse knowledge, and the model described earlier would increase that. It is not possible to de-contextualise assessment but local teacher-led assessment makes it possible to minimise the use of contexts which will have a detrimental effect on pupils' opportunities for achievement.

So the objections to assessment by teachers based on issues of validity and reliability can be overcome. The next question is the frequency of national assessment. The present key stage tests are of little use for the individual pupil. On the contrary, they are widely seen as damaging, including by many parents. The conclusion to be drawn is that there should be no national testing system prior to the terminal stage of compulsory schooling. Incidentally, this fits with the original vision of the Task Group on Assessment and Testing for an assessment system designed for formative purposes to meet all the needs of national assessment prior to age-16 with summative assessment occurring from age-16 onwards[15].

However, there is a clear need for a standard assessment at the end of compulsory schooling, which as explained earlier is viewed here to occur from age-16 onwards. There are strong arguments for offering providers of education and training post age-16 and employers a standard school-leavers' certification. Of course, accreditation of skills, including all the practical and soft skills wanted by employers, will be much more useful than the general measure of academic ability provided by differentiated GCSE outcomes.

The postponement of national testing, and the selection which goes with it, may seem to be a radical proposition. However, international evidence now clearly links high pupil achievement with systems that postpone national assessment and selection. Finland's education system is a prime example of this as it gained top ranking scores in maths, problem solving, science and reading in the OECD Programme for International Student Achievement (PISA) surveys of 2000 and 2003. Finland defers national testing until a terminal stage. In fact, not only did Finland's students score highly in terms of performance and proficiency, they demonstrated positive attitudes towards learning as this excerpt from the Executive Summary of the 2003 survey indicates: "For example, more than half of the students in France and Japan report that they get very tense when they have to do mathematics homework, but only seven percent of students in Finland and the Netherlands report this. It is noteworthy that Finland and the Netherlands are also two of the top performing countries[16]."

It is worth restating that the association between external assessment and selection is deeply embedded within this country's education culture. The current system may not look like a selection system, but it is perceived as such by pupils. The totemic importance of level 4 at key stage 2 is now so huge that pupils who fail to achieve it cannot be blamed for feeling just that – failures. And we know that this is just how many of them do feel. We also know the effect this has on their future attitudes to learning. No wonder there is a dip in performance between year 6 and 7. The policy of a differentiated offer post age-14 makes the key stage 3 tests an even clearer selection mechanism, determining how pupils' 'choice' is to be 'guided'.

Some commentators argue that these tests are good training for a competitive world. This argument does not seem to stand up for those successful nations like Finland which inhabit the same competitive world. Neither would it make sense to any trainer, who would not enter their protegee for any competition until they were fully developed and ready. A rational assessment system for schools delays formal external testing until necessary. If the nation wishes to maximise the achievement of all pupils it will avoid a culture of competition in which losers become demotivated or disengaged. It will also give teachers the space to use assessment as a key part of learning, a central activity for teacher and pupil within a low-stakes context.

There may need to be an exception to this system, for largely political reasons. The counter-productive obsession of British governments with a few highly important skills was discussed earlier. However much it may be deprecated, this obsession is a reality, and so is its adoption by other sections of society, including, from time to time, employers' organisations. The skills, often termed core skills but sometimes labelled as something else, are English, maths, and IT competency. The definitions and syllabuses vary with each successive policy aimed at greater emphasis.

In order to comply with this longstanding political imperative, and to allay the parental fears it has created, it may be necessary to implement new national tests in these subjects, perhaps based on recent development work. Using the Scottish bank method, they could be offered to pupils on a when-ready basis. To meet the country's apparent need for reassurance, the tests should be offered at one level only, the level being that of functional competence. Some pupils might pass the test perhaps in year 4, others in year 9 or beyond.

Apart from the tests of core skills, AFL will be the primary method of assessment throughout the career of pupils in a league-table free environment. Definitions of assessment for learning centre on its purpose and focus; AFL is any assessment for which the first priority in its design and practice is the promotion of pupils' future learning, thus differing from assessment designed primarily for purposes of accountability, ranking, or of certifying competence[17]. Teachers using an AFL approach will work with learners to gather and interpret evidence to discover where they are in their learning, where they need to go and how best to get there.

AFL is no stranger to the education policy agenda; the advent of 'personalised learning' has brought it to the fore where it is seen as a powerful means of helping teachers to tailor their teaching to pupils to get best improvement, and to involve, motivate and help them to take the next steps in learning. Certainly, AFL is an approach which has the learning needs of individual students at its heart and one which involves students far more directly in the assessment process.

Fortunately there is an abundance of evidence in the UK and across several countries to demonstrate the positive effects of formative assessment, even within the current system. If only all initiatives in education had such a strong body of evidence to support a claim to raise standards! Research has found that an increased focus on using formative assessment as principle and practice within the classroom produced gains in pupil achievement, even when measured in narrow terms such as national curriculum tests and examinations[17]. AFL, with its formative assessment focus, has a positive impact on summative results to the tune of a quarter to a half GCSE grade improvement per student[17]. However, research also points to the tension between AFL and summative assessment[17].

All this will require a culture change in schools and in the wider community about how we view achievement in schools. Many pupils and their parents will see learning tasks as competitions, achievement marked by a grade or a ranking within the class. One of the key problems with this view is that there will always be losers as well as winners and those who have a track record of losing will not even try; better to be seen as lazy or bored than stupid or a loser. Teachers working with researchers on formative assessment methods have found that whilst pupils' learning can be advanced through feedback in the form of comments, the giving of marks or grades has a negative effect as pupils then ignore the feedback where also given[17]. Once grades were removed, pupils concentrated on the comment given by the teacher and on how it could help them improve.

We also know that:

- pupils told that 'feedback will help you to learn' learn more than those told that 'how you do tells us how smart you are and what grades you'll get'; the difference is greatest for low achievers;
- those given feedback as marks are likely to see it as a way of comparing themselves with others (ego-involvement), those given only comments see it as helping them to improve (task-involvement): the latter group then out-performs the former;
- in a competitive system, low achievers attribute their performance to lack of 'ability', high achievers to their effort; in a task-oriented system effort and learning is improved, particularly amongst low achievers[17].

At present, our learners are often passive recipients of knowledge, spending much of their time in the classroom practising passive revision techniques. Formative assessment techniques will demand of them a far more active role with a corresponding development of understanding of their own learning. Indeed, key to AFL is the self-assessment of pupils; in order for pupils to properly achieve a learning goal they need to understand it and assess what is required to attain it. And teachers will be their partners in pursuit of this shared goal, working with them on the journey of exploration and development of ideas in which learning pupils will be involved.

In a system built upon AFL the teacher's role changes significantly from the constrictive one of test-coach which dominates when a summative testing regime is the foundation of the system. For teachers to be empowered to encourage and enable pupils to be participants in their own learning, their efforts must be valued, respected and trusted. The latter requirement is perhaps the strongest in the current climate of excessive accountability.

Literature and research around AFL yield a rich source of support, information and advice to teachers, through research observations, case studies and exemplifications of good practice. It would be crucial that teachers are supported until they become familiar with it, through training and resource provision. Each school needs to be an assessment community where assessment is placed at the heart of each pupil's, each class's and each department's curriculum.

The problem with assessment is to persuade the politicians that thinking has moved on, and to provide them with a narrative which allows them to abandon national testing graciously and to replace it with a fit-for-purpose terminal assessment and different forms of teacher and school accountability. The Government needs to understand how the provision of training and support for teachers could create confidence in a different curriculum and assessment regime. In the next chapter the implicatons for teachers are considered.

References

1 Swaffield, S. and Dudley, P. 2002. *Assessment Literacy for Wise Decisions*. London, Association of Teachers and Lecturers.

2 Assessment Reform Group. 2006. *Assessment Systems for the Future, Working Paper 1: Aims and outcomes of the first year's work of the project*. Draft paper 10. London, Assessment Reform Group.

3 Newton, P.E. 2006. *Clarifying the purposes of educational assessment*. Draft paper June 2006. London, QCA.

4 Assessment Reform Group. 2006. *The role of teachers in the assessment of learning*. London, Assessment Reform Group.

5 Harlen, W. 2004. *Can assessment by teachers be a dependable option for summative purposes?* Published in *Perspectives on pupil assessment* by the General Teaching Council. London, General Teaching Council.

6 Wiliam, D. 2001. *Level best? Levels of attainment in national curriculum assessment*. London, Association of Teachers and Lecturers.

7 Webb, R. and Vulliamy, G. 2006. *Coming full circle: The impact of New Labour's education policies on primary school teachers' work*. London, Association of Teachers and Lecturers.

8 OfSTED. 2005. *Primary National Strategy: An evaluation of its impact in primary schools*. London, Her Majesty's Stationary Office.

9 Daugherty *et al*. 2004. *Learning pathways through statutory assessment: Key stages 2 and 3. Final Report*. London, Assessment Review Group.

10 Beverton *et al*. 2005. *Teaching approaches to promote consistent level 4 performance in Key Stage 2 English and mathematics*. Durham, University of Durham, School of Education.

11 OfSTED. 2002. *Changing schools: effectiveness of transfer arrangements at age 11, an evaluation by OfSTED*. London, Her Majesty's Stationary Office.

12 Wilmut, J. 2004. *Experiences of summative teacher assessment in the UK*. London, QCA.

13 General Teaching Council. 2004. *The role of teacher in pupil assessment*. Published in *Perspectives on pupil assessment* by the General Teaching Council. London, General Teaching Council.

14 Gipps, C. and Stobart, G. 2004. *Fairness in Assessment*. Published in *Perspectives on pupil assessment* by the General Teaching Council. London, General Teaching Council.

15 National Curriculum Task Group on Assessment and Testing. 1988. *A report 1988*. Department of Education and Science. London, Her Majesty's Stationary Office.

16 Organisation for Economic Co-operation and Development. 2004. *Learning for tomorrow's world: First results from PISA 2003: Executive Summary*. France, OECD.

17 Black *et al*. 2002. *Working Inside the Black Box*. London, King's College, Department of Education and Professional Studies.

CHAPTER SEVEN

Teaching is for teachers

Are you crazy? Are you seriously trying to tell us the thing we need in schools is more change? Thus the longstanding plea of teachers in England, and a possible response to the proposals for substantial changes to the curriculum and its associated assessment. It is true that the demand for stability is the loudest and most consistent cry from school staff, not excluding school leaders and their organisations. In this chapter we examine this demand in more detail and show why our proposals are not only what the profession needs but what it will want when it understands them.

This is not the place for a history of the teaching workforce, but it would be as well to recall in outline the circumstances which led to its present situation. As we have seen, in the mid eighties the dominating characteristic of the teaching workforce in the public mind was of bloody-minded discontent. The Government resolved longstanding rumbling on pay and conditions by abolishing the negotiating machinery, later establishing an independent pay review body. Before the profession had time to recover from this affront the Education Reform Bill was upon it. Although there was a consensus in favour of a national curriculum the profession was outraged by the institution of market mechanisms, regular external national testing and intrusive external inspection. In addition, teachers in London also had to deal with the abolition of the Inner London Education Authority.

This created the dominant mood of teachers in the nineties, which could be described as sullen compliance. Overall, teachers resented the loss of autonomy and the imposition of new accountabilities, not least because they created demands for additional work.

Since teachers' initial response to proposals for change is usually, 'what about the workload?' it is necessary to examine this issue carefully. It is worth remembering that however much teachers protested about the curriculum and assessment in the early nineties for ideological reasons technically the dispute was about workload. The context was a teachers' contract with effectively no limit to the hours of work. By the end of the nineties, pressure from union members alerted the teaching unions to the problem, who in turn pressured the Government into action. The resultant government commissioned research demonstrated that teachers worked upon average in excess of 50 hours per week. Eventually, in 2003 an agreement was signed by most teaching unions to engage in joint work with the Government and employers on workload reduction and workforce reform. To date, average weekly working time has reduced by more than two hours.

Evidence shows that teachers enter the profession largely from a commitment to children and young people; like some other professions the job is a moral enterprise. It is therefore unlikely, and indeed is not the case, for teachers as a group to be work-shy. This adds to the complication of the workload question; left to their own devices many teachers would work very long hours. What teachers want, and the education system needs, is to be able to make their own decisions about how they spend their time.

Teachers want to prepare lessons but do not want to spend hours writing lesson plans. Many other tasks currently undertaken are unwanted because teachers judge that they add nothing to the quality of their work or their pupils' learning experiences. Often, the tasks are derived from one or other of the accountability mechanisms that swamp schools. For example, the Government insists that performance in external tests is the way to measure the quality of schools. As a result, teachers are answerable in their schools for the performance of their pupils in these tests. But even if they are successful in those terms they are still required to provide detailed evidence of the planning and execution of the lessons which produce the success, with a high degree of monitoring. It is excessive and unnecessary. It simply does not make sense for them to be answerable in detail in addition to the steps they take to achieve those pupil outcomes, unless those outcomes are unsatisfactory.

One very widely shared characteristic of teachers is their cynicism about the role of the Government, often represented as a lack of trust. Almost all teachers accept the principle of accountability but complain about the duplication. Most teachers sooner or later come to question whether the curriculum and assessment system meets their pupils' needs.

Inevitably, the work of classroom teachers is particularly intensive and exhausting. Contact with pupils has the intensity of a theatre performance and teachers are tightly bound by school timetables. The additional stress of negative interaction with uncooperative children is an additional factor. But pupil contact occupies only one half of the working week. The essence of the workload question is therefore not the amount of work but the control of work, especially during the other half of the working week. Under the current conditions of prescribed curriculum, assessment, pedagogy and monitoring teachers resent the deprivation of agency; the removal of their rights to exercise their professional judgment. Some commentators describe this process as de-skilling, others as reducing the teacher to a technician, but all refer to the same issue: that teachers should be permitted to make decisions about the curriculum, assessment and pedagogy. However, currently, such decisions remain under the control of the Government.

In the long run, a model of good practice involving central imposition is untenable. Teaching should be both a learning and an innovating profession, and the Government's role should be to recognise and optimise the spread of good practice arising from classrooms. Local communities of teachers should be equipped to reflect on their practice and to try out new ways of improving learning. After all, all models of good practice have a starting point somewhere. The national bank of expertise will decline unless changes are made to restore proper autonomy so as to encourage teachers to make their own judgments on appropriate curriculum, assessment and pedagogy. The country needs a cadre of experts in these matters, not least to staff various national agencies, but the current generation of experts arose in an era where they had space. Where will the next generation of experts come from unless today's teachers are provided with the same space? Recently, the National Strategies changed tack and became far less prescriptive, but the message has been slow to reach most schools. We know that when the Government first tried to address the issue by giving successful schools 'the power to innovate', almost all applicant schools identified freedoms they already possessed, unknowingly because of an aura of central imposition created by government.

When the Government introduced the concept 'new professionalism' as an aspect of its policy on school workforce reform, terms like 'autonomy' or 'agency' did not appear. It consisted of stronger management of teachers to ensure that they undertook continuing professional development and that their performance was related to pay progression. For ATL, however, new professionalism must mean giving back to teachers autonomy in professional matters, together with a rationalised set of accountability mechanisms.

This view of new professionalism conceptualises teachers as lead professionals who are equipped and empowered to take forward the curriculum debate within their schools. The Government must intensify activity in support of more shared leadership within schools, greater commitment to staff development and the creation of a culture of innovation that must generalise good practice and eliminate bad. With the implementation of such policies, the collective intellectual power of the teaching workforce will be recognised as a major national asset and utilised to create a more vibrant education system.

If this kind of new professionalism were to be introduced the workload issue would be transformed. Teachers would regard themselves, and be regarded by their leaders, as skilled professionals capable of planning and prioritising the use of their time outside the classroom, whilst being subject to sensible accountability arrangements. A consequence of this would be more balanced responses to new initiatives. This is the context in which we now consider the workload impact of the changes to the curriculum and assessment proposed earlier.

It must be accepted that if the design and the detail of the curriculum and associated assessment were handed over to teachers tomorrow there would be grumble, grumble, grumble. It is vital that these changes follow the restoration of teachers' sense of agency. However, the likely impact of the proposals, particularly regarding assessment, on working time can easily be over-estimated. In order to consider this it is necessary to understand the amount of time spent on assessment at present.

A teacher working with a group of pupils spends a substantial amount of time in preparing them for external assessment. Although this varies according to the year group, when setting, marking practice tests or test questions and individual and group coaching are factored in on top of the teaching timetable the load starts to become clear. It has been estimated that year 6 class teachers spend on average 400 hours per year on assessment activities. In years 7, 8 and 9, it is approximately 100 hours per class for subject teachers.

This vast amount of work is not valued by most teachers as they do not like the idea of using a pressure cooker to produce test results. In the proposed curriculum, whilst the assessment and recording of skills will take time they will be conducted largely in class and will be easy to complete, it is therefore likely that it will take less time than the current demands associated with external assessment. Teacher morale will rise as a result.

Beyond doubt, primary school teachers will feel their load lightened. In most schools, the abolition of the end of year tests in key stage 2 will reduce the pressure. Secondary school teachers will have the load from coaching and marking coursework or its replacement 'controlled assessment'. Secondary school teachers currently feel obliged to test frequently in years 10 and 11, thus increasing their marking load. They also feel obliged to spend additional hours outside normal lessons to provide individual and group coaching. Like their primary school colleagues they perceive this not only as extra work but as a loss of control, and therefore an attack on their professionalism; few believe this kind of teaching meets the needs of their pupils.

Under the model described in Chapter 6, year 11 teachers would undertake assessments. It would be less time consuming than current practice for the preparation of written exams. So, whilst secondary school teachers may currently believe that teacher assessment is to be avoided because it is time consuming, they will eventually realise that their working lives will benefit in terms of improved quality and shorter working hours when they consider the implications of the abolition of the current key stage testing arrangements. Primary school teachers will also appreciate these benefits if they are freed from all necessity for external test preparation.

Assessment is only one part of the new responsibilities for teachers derived from a locally determined curriculum. Another significant component is that of curriculum design. Would teachers in each school be expected to begin with a skills map and a blank piece of paper? This would be a colossal task and one for which many schools would feel ill-prepared. There is, however, another much more likely scenario.

As the new curriculum is developed and approved many agencies will be involved in the design of workable models for schools. Assuming the Government retains the QCA, it will be at the forefront of producing these models. (Incidentally, there would be good arguments for the retention of the QCA, not least because there will still be a national curriculum and a nationally overseen system of skills assessment at school leaving age). The QCA may produce model syllabuses in a range of subjects derivable from the skills list and other models based on different forms of organisation of learning, such as model cross-curricular projects. Other national agencies may do the same thing. We can imagine a range of interest groups offering part syllabuses and resources based on their particular interests. LAs, or in some cases consortia of authorities, will then offer their own versions. If earlier arguments are valid, they will differ to a greater or lesser degree according to local circumstances. Lastly, some individual schools, or collaboratives of schools, will be confident enough to design their own models and make them available to others.

Most schools are likely to start down the road to autonomy by selecting one of the many models on offer. They may well then modify them immediately or as their confidence grows, but they will be prepared to review their model and ensure it works for their pupils. They will also be creative in reaching their own solutions.

It cannot be denied that the move to a new curriculum will entail additional work, even if the new one is taken off the peg by choice rather than imposed or created by the school. It will be necessary to carefully phase in the introduction of the new curriculum, bearing in mind workload implications. However, underneath it all must be the assumption that for most teachers this will be a labour of love. They will willingly undertake the necessary hours to replace a system they despise with one they created for themselves and their pupils.

Such developments will require demanding changes for both initial teacher education and continuing training; they will take some time to work through and implement. From the comparatively simple but ultimately unsatisfying requirement to learn the national curriculum and its assessment arrangements, trainee and serving teachers alike will need to confront the deep issues regarding the purpose of education and the learning needs of pupils. They will need to consider the issues raised in this book and more.

As mentioned earlier, secondary subject enthusiasts will need to work through the integration of their subject skills into the new curriculum. They will become champions for their subjects and guardians of their subject skills. Very possibly some of the model secondary curricula will continue a subject-based timetable with skills mapped onto it, as tried by Govan High school. Other models will have different kinds of timetable, perhaps with class teachers or teaching teams. In these cases, the subject leaders will have the additional responsibility of ensuring that staff are equipped to develop subject skills through their teaching. Let's be frank: not all of this will be accepted by some secondary school teachers of academic subjects. Their arguments, however, will lack one key component: the ability to take a balanced perspective on the real learning needs of all school leavers in today's world.

In this chapter, we have looked at three main concerns that teachers might have regarding the adoption of a locally determined curriculum: the workload implications, the training implications and the impact on academic subject teaching. On the one hand, teachers say that the last thing they need is more change. On the other, teachers say that the current curriculum and testing regime is not fit for purpose. If it is the case that the overarching demand from teachers is a sense of appropriate professional agency in their work then the majority will welcome change that gives them the right to make decisions on curriculum, pedagogy and assessment. Given the necessary support and training, they will also be enthusiastic about the work of implementing their decisions. It will probably be less time-consuming, and certainly less onerous, than their present duties.

One thing is certain. No curriculum can be taught without the consent of teachers, sullen or committed. Out there, in staffrooms around the country, teachers are approaching the end of their consent for the present arrangements. They know they are doing their pupils a disservice, and they want something better. A debate around the proposals in this book will lead us to that better place.

CHAPTER EIGHT

Subject to change

This book argues that society needs a different school curriculum. We also need to emphasise why the Government needs a different curriculum. Most of all, let's remember why our children and young people need a different curriculum.

Concern about the current state of childhood might be a contribution to a major new direction in social attitudes, or it might just be a moral panic. Is your glass half empty or half full? On the one hand, despite the deep inequalities within modern Britain most children are bigger, stronger and more capable than their predecessors. With their ability to keep up with IT developments they have an unprecedented capacity to access information. But they are less active, less disciplined, and if we maintain the distinction between information and knowledge, possibly less knowledgeable than previous generations.

There are other worrying indicators. The mental health of teenagers becomes ever more problematic. Suicide is the second most common cause of death for 15–24 year-olds. This was another five-minute media wonder when UNICEF published its international comparison of childhood happiness, with Britain 'at the bottom of the league'. School staff are at the front line, identifying problems, seeking treatment and continuing to support pupils. The reasons for these phenomena are clearly complex and deep-seated but many teachers would argue that children's experience of school is a contributing factor.

We know that in many schools there is a pressured atmosphere in classrooms. Teachers are anxious about test performance and meeting targets and their anxiety is transmitted to their pupils. In many classrooms, teaching is overtly directed towards tests to a much greater degree than in the pre-SATs era. We know that tests demotivate those who struggle to achieve and that they attack self-esteem. As argued earlier, it is not the case that it is only low achievers who suffer in this system. All pupils get the message that test outcome is more important than learning. They also expect teachers to take responsibility for laying success on a plate; just follow the detailed instructions, no skill needed. This is how successful pupils come to adopt highly instrumental attitudes to education.

This is no way to bring up children. This is no way to produce young people with self-confidence, security and curiosity about the world. This is no way to run an education system.

It needs to be repeated: not all schools or teachers are like this. This book contains examples of schools that have sought another way and there are many others doing the same. Many teachers produce sparkling lessons that enthuse and motivate their pupils. When Ofsted says that the quality of teaching has never been higher it is not referring just to the 'standard' lesson format, which is efficient, if boring, and chilling in its conformity. Ofsted inspectors see many inspiring lessons but they are not the norm.

Today's parents tend to be strong supporters of their own children's schools, even if they do not believe schools in general are doing a good job. However, they must be aware of the lack of enthusiasm for learning displayed by their offspring. They must see that their children learn little, in the sense that they quickly forget what they learnt for the test. They must understand that the certificates their children receive at the end of it all are no more than a passport to the next hurdle and do not signify the acquisition of much useful skill.

This is where politicians are out of touch. They are unwilling to contemplate substantial changes to the curriculum or qualifications because they fear the changes would be unpopular. They would be unpopular with some; particularly those who have derived most benefit themselves from the present arrangements and those who identify ideologically with high status forms of knowledge. Many more people, however, including many parents, know that something is wrong in today's classrooms. Many would prefer that children learnt useful things. Many would like schools to spend more time on communication and social skills. Many would like a more practical curriculum as long as it does not disadvantage their children.

At the beginning of this book, we described how the Government was facing policy problems for which curriculum and assessment reform is the answer. However much money the Government throws at the problem of the range of achievement it will not close the gap as the system is based on selection, rejection and the creation of failure. The only credible explanation for the continuing refusal to make the connection and the necessary policy adjustment is timidity. In no other policy area would successive governments refuse to consider modernising a system that was more than a century old.

The Government would not be leaping into the unknown if it decided to adopt a locally built curriculum with little national assessment. Although international comparisons come with substantial health warnings some of the most successful education systems in the world are based on this model. Finland is the outstanding case, and the

Government has sent many envoys there to seek the secrets of its success. The secret is that it ensures a high quality teaching force, allows them to get on with it, and operates a fully non-selective school system.

Despite this, it was with scandalous timidity that the Government rejected the reforms proposed by Tomlinson in 2004. Tomlinson constructed a model for 14–19 so expertly that it was legitimately all things to all people. For many its strength was an improved vocational pathway; of course, this book argues that we need a single entitlement for all until the school leaving age, but there were clear possibilities for a more comprehensive model. It was so expert that Tomlinson built a wide consensus for his proposals, and it was only the last minute turnaround by the CBI that broke the unanimity and gave the Government the space to take the conservative decision. It must be remembered that the proposals which produced this consensus implied the eventual demise of both GCSE and 'A' level, or at least their incorporation into the Diploma. The Tomlinson episode demonstrates that it would be possible to gain wide support for the abolition of GCSE, as we propose.

There is one other major policy line which stands between the Government and assessment reform. Test results are an important part of the accountability framework for schools. We have shown, however, that they are fatally flawed because of their lack of reliability. Neither are they necessary for this purpose. Schools are subject to a large number of accountability mechanisms; they overlap. Together they are excessive and inefficient and fail to provide accountability to those who deserve it because they are directed towards central government. The Government could cut out some of the duplication by ending the use of test results for this purpose without losing its firm grip on school performance.

It would be completely erroneous for supporters of the status quo to argue that teachers and their supporters are trying to avoid accountability by opposing national tests. The requirement to be accountable is not in question; the question is about proper forms of accountability.

We have to admit that our proposals would require a major change in the Government's narrative. But it is worth repeating that they are entirely in tune with other aspects of the narrative. Often, ministers talk about social justice when seeking policies to equalise pupil performance. Downing Street has been concerned that at the end of the twentieth century the rate of social mobility was lower than in previous generations. Improving the school performance, self-esteem and employability of our lowest achievers is an essential (but on its own insufficient) condition for a fairer society. Ministers need to ask deeper questions about how to achieve this; more of the same will not do it. They need to consider how performance should be measured in the information age, and realise that much wider definitions are necessary, as suggested in this book. Once employed, these new definitions should enable those who are currently unsuccessful to prosper. A local curriculum responsive to community need will allow even the suspicious and angry to work through their feelings and learn the value of learning.

The most important change of thinking on the part of the Government would need to be its attitude to centralised control. The evidence is overwhelming that in the longer term direct Whitehall control over professional decisions is an ineffective strategy. From time to time, the need to devolve decision-making in public services is recognised, shortly after which another piece of micro-management is announced. Ministers' repeated attempts to second guess the profession in their choice of books for the English

Literature syllabus is a prime example. Politicians also want to impose their view on how reading should be taught but they don't know how to teach children to read so they should leave it to the professionals.

The proposed national curriculum would leave the Government with less control over the detail of what is taught. But being a statutory curriculum the Government would still control the required skills outcomes; the Government answers the big questions about the aims of the curriculum, whilst the implementation is put in local hands. This is a description of good governance.

The Government must also think through the difference between entitlement and uniformity. Under the proposals there would be less uniformity in terms of the knowledge acquired by pupils. This would be a good thing: not only would pupils be likely to remember more because of the more active pedagogy and their increased ownership of learning, but the total national stock of knowledge would increase. The entitlement for all pupils would be to the skills they need. The Government would remain the mediator between competing interests for a place in the statutory curriculum, but because a new national curriculum would need to be designed from first principles its decisions would have more impact than the blanket acceptance of tradition that took place first time round.

So, the Government needs our curriculum and assessment reforms because it cannot meet its goals for raising the achievement of the least successful learners. Neither can it meet its aspirations for a future workforce with the skills wanted by employers. Ultimately, the motive for these proposals is not to support this or any government but to ensure our society gets the education it needs and pays for.

We know that most people work in schools from vocation. They believe in the power of education. They want to help children develop into young people with self-belief, optimism, a commitment to making the best of themselves and the skills and understanding to achieve this. They try to instil in the next generation a belief in honesty and in the value in caring for others, and a belief in working together for the benefit of all. For too many of our children, they provide the only security in their lives.

These same education professionals also say, whenever anyone bothers to listen: our children need something better than their present learning diet. Yes, our children need the essential literacy and numeracy skills, but those who struggle with them need a different kind of learning opportunity to acquire them. And yes, the constant teach and test regime prevents us from exploring in places our pupils want to go. We struggle to see the whole child when we're told to look at the target and want the flexibility to give our pupils the learning experiences that engage and inspire them to go further. We want to give them practice in useful skills, such as social skills, which will enable them to be successful citizens in our ever more complex world, and manual skills, which can lead to the deep satisfaction of creativity. We want to create opportunities for success, not the certainty of failure.

This is the moral purpose of schools and the social purpose which is vital to the future of our society. And this is currently subverted by a narrow-minded concentration on learning facts, testing them and forgetting them.

In this book, we have given a number of examples of the many schools in England that are heroically trying to subvert the system and to provide learning opportunities which suit their pupils. Now the QCA has endorsed this rebellion with the new flexibility built into key stage 3. But we need more. We need large-scale system change to enable all schools to copy them.

First though, we need a bigger public and popular debate on these issues. This book has tried to make a contribution. No doubt, it has enraged many readers. Some will find it wishy-washy, others will see it as heralding the end of civilisation. Please find your voice and use it. We don't want the debate conducted through the politician's sound bite; we want a prolonged and serious discussion on the way forward for curriculum and assessment in our schools. Will the ideas in this book stand up to scrutiny? It would be surprising if there did not need to be some adjustment at least. All we say is, let's have proper scrutiny, not the swapping of commonplace insults. Let's agree the future for our young people needs that proper debate. But let's all agree on one thing: the present curriculum must be subject to change.